# CONTENTS

# CRUEL KINGS AND MEAN QUEENS FAMILY TREE

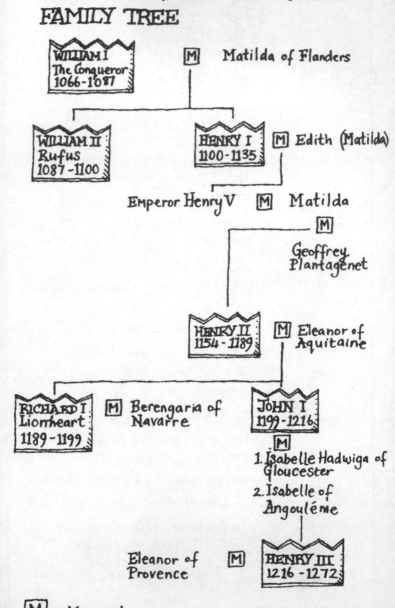

WILLIAM I The Conqueror 1066-1087 · M · Matilda of Flanders

WILLIAM II Rufus 1087-1100

HENRY I 1100-1135 · M · Edith (Matilda)

Emperor Henry V · M · Matilda

· M · Geoffrey Plantagenet

HENRY II 1154-1189 · M · Eleanor of Aquitaine

RICHARD I Lionheart 1189-1199 · M · Berengaria of Navarre

JOHN I 1199-1216 · M ·
1. Isabelle Hadwiga of Gloucester
2. Isabelle of Angoulême

Eleanor of Provence · M · HENRY III 1216-1272

M = Married

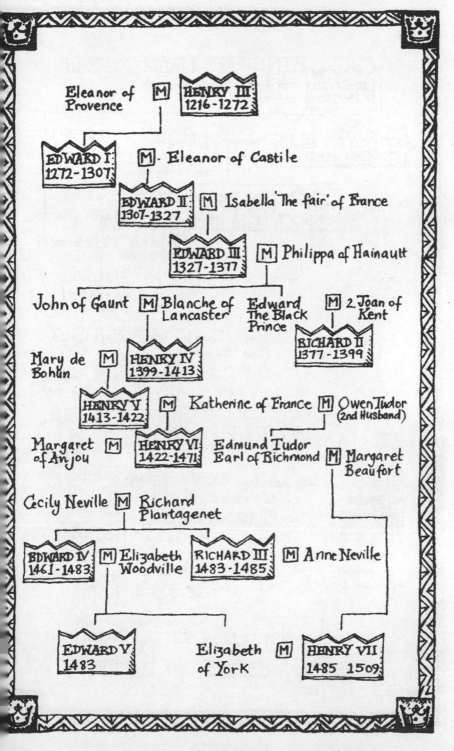

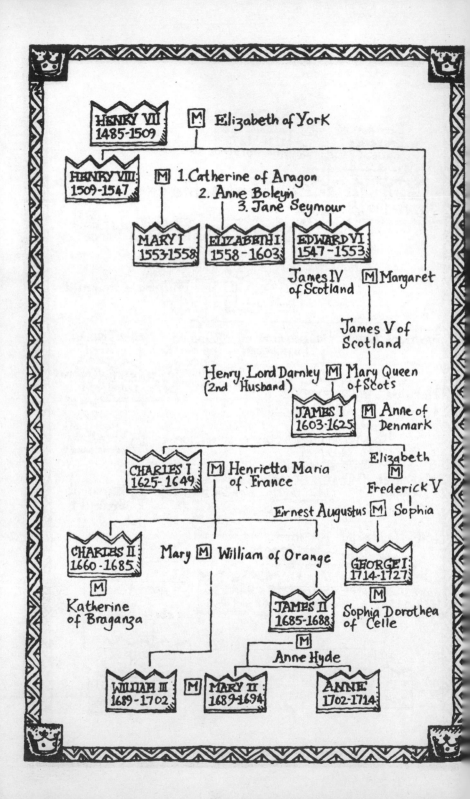

**HENRY VII**
1485-1509 Ⓜ Elizabeth of York

**HENRY VIII**
1509-1547 Ⓜ 1. Catherine of Aragon
2. Anne Boleyn
3. Jane Seymour

**MARY I**
1553-1558

**ELIZABETH I**
1558-1603

**EDWARD VI**
1547-1553

James IV
of Scotland Ⓜ Margaret

James V of
Scotland

Henry, Lord Darnley
(2nd Husband) Ⓜ Mary Queen
of Scots

**JAMES I**
1603-1625 Ⓜ Anne of
Denmark

**CHARLES I**
1625-1649 Ⓜ Henrietta Maria
of France

Elizabeth
Ⓜ
Frederick V

Ernest Augustus Ⓜ Sophia

**CHARLES II**
1660-1685 Mary Ⓜ William of Orange

**GEORGE I**
1714-1727

Ⓜ

Katherine
of Braganza

**JAMES II**
1685-1688

Sophia Dorothea
of Celle

Ⓜ

Anne Hyde

**WILLIAM III**
1689-1702 Ⓜ **MARY II**
1689-1694

**ANNE**
1702-1714

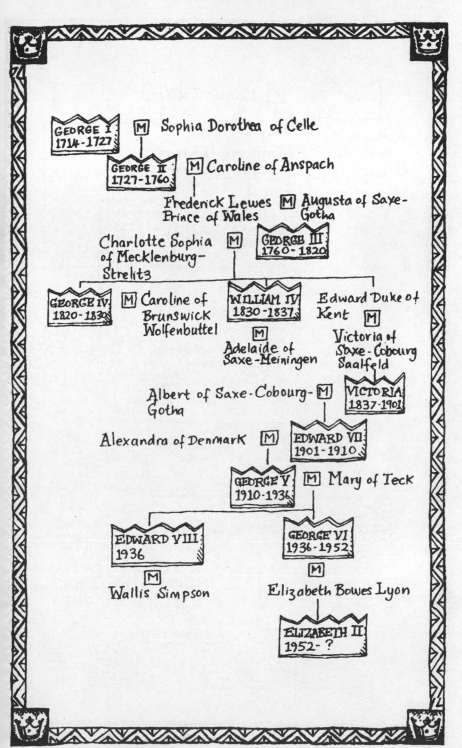

# Introduction

Some history books tell you about great kings and grand queens. But this is a *horrible* history. This will tell you about grotty kings and gruesome queens. From their disgusting habits (like James I)...

...to their dreadful deaths. As the famous poet Shakespeare said in the play, *Richard II*...

*Let us sit upon the ground
And tell sad stories of the death of kings –
How some have been deposed, some slain in war,
Some haunted by the ghosts they have deposed,
Some poisoned by their wives, some sleeping killed.
All murdered.*

And there are enough of those 'sad stories' to keep you sitting on the ground till your bum is numb! And not just sad stories. Funny ones, incredible ones and plain daft ones.

Britain has had as weird a collection of kings and queens as any country. And a lot of their stories are in this book.

11

The foul facts…

The funny facts…

The fantastic facts…

So! What are you waiting for?

# Monarchs of the murky past

A monk called Geoffrey of Monmouth wrote the first *History of the Kings of Britain* in the 1100s. Old Geoff *said* he got the information from a *certain very ancient book written in the British language.*

Now Geoff was a monk and a holy man, but it has to be said ... he told *fibs*! Not little fibs but dirty great whacking *lies*. Most of his stories are fairy tales and invention. For example...

- You probably know how the Greeks beat the Trojans with the famous Wooden Horse trick. Geoffrey said that the Trojan hero Aeneas fled the burning city and escaped. His great-grandson, Brutus, sailed off to find some islands called Albion and become their king. Brutus renamed the islands after himself ... so Brutus-land became Bruton became Britain.

- Brutus found giants living in the islands of Albion. (That explains Stonehenge – not a temple but giants' cricket stumps!) Brutus killed the giants and took over. His children and their families reigned over Britain for the next thousand years.

- One early king, Bladud, was cured of leprosy when he fell in some magic mud – then he learnt to fly.

- Princes Ferrex and Porrux argued with each other as to who should take over the throne of their father, Gorboduc. Porrux killed Ferrex in an outburst of brotherly love – so their mum, Queen Judon, killed Porrux.

That was Geoffrey's story. The *truth* is that the British Isles were inhabited by Celtic people from eastern Europe –

not Trojans. When the Romans arrived there were lots of tribes, each with its own little king or queen. At least we know these Brit leaders really existed. People like the leader of the Iceni, Boudica.

*Did you know…?*
Boudica died in AD 62 after failing to beat the Romans. (One report said she had poisoned herself to avoid capture.) Archaeologists say her grave is somewhere under Platform 8 of London's Kings Cross railway station. You would think she'd be resting peacefully now, wouldn't you? But, in the early 1900s, she was seen driving two phantom horses through the Lincolnshire village of Cammeringham. Of all the ghost reports of all the British leaders in history, Boudica's spook must be the oldest.

**The Dark Ages**
After the Romans left, the history of Britain becomes uncertain again. The only people keeping records were the monks – and they kept having those records destroyed by invaders like the Awful Angles, Savage Saxons and Vicious Vikings.

So we're back to old Geoffrey's fairy tales for a lot of those years. Was there really a King Arthur? Did he really pull swords from stones, meet ladies in lakes and have a round table? No one knows for certain.

There certainly *was* a King *Alfred*, though. And he began to keep historical records again. He was the king of a bit of Britain in the south west – called Wessex.

Alfred's family and the ones who followed all tried to take more of England from the Vikings. Harold almost did it. Then along came two invasions to finish him off. First came the Vikings in the north, but Harold beat them. Then the Normans in the south. Harry hurried to meet them, but an arrow in the eye saw him off.

So the first king to claim to rule all of England was one who came over from France. The Norman, William the Conqueror...

# William I (1066–1087) – William the Conker

## Claim to fame
- Won the Battle of Hastings in 1066.
- Built castles around England and put his barons in them to keep an eye on the English.
- Had the *Domesday Book* written so he could charge lots of lovely taxes. (Of course, *William* didn't have to pay those taxes).

## Cruel king
William the Conqueror did not believe in the old saying, 'Forgive and forget'. Shortly after he was crowned there was

a rebellion in the north of England where hundreds of his Normans were killed. A twelfth-century history said…

*William fell on the English in the North like a lion on its prey. He ordered that their houses, food, tools and belongings should be burnt and large herds of their cattle should be butchered. Thousands of children, old people, young men and women died of starvation.*

But fate plays strange tricks. The French king made some nasty remarks about William being too fat. We had another Billy fury. 'I'll set the whole of France ablaze!' Big Bill threatened.

He started by setting fire to the castle at Mantes. But, as the fire burned, sparks flew in the air. Billy's horse stepped on a hot cinder and stumbled. The conqueror fell forward on to the point of his saddle and did himself a nasty injury – probably burst his bladder. He died in agony.

**Funny fact**
William the Conqueror had the famous *Domesday Book* written. It listed all of the places in the kingdom and all of the wealth – so the king could tax that wealth. You couldn't argue with it. It was law until the end of the world. Till Doomsday, in fact. That's how it got its nickname. But, did you know, William never read the *Domesday Book*. Why not?
1  He died before it was finished.
2  He tried to borrow a copy but the library was closed.
3  William couldn't read.

**Fantastic fact**

William the Conqueror was so strong that he could jump on to his horse when dressed in full armour.

**Foul fact**

William the Conqueror was a pretty big bloke. That was one of the problems that turned his funeral into a disaster… or a farce.

- His body went mouldy quickly. Two of the undertakers caught a fever from the corpse and died.
- As he was carried to his monastery tomb a fire broke out. The mourners put the coffin down and went to fight the fire.
- A man interrupted the funeral shouting that William had stolen the monastery land and had no right to be buried there. (The man was given money to shut him up!)

17

- A stone tomb was made for him after his death. But he was large, and the body swelled a lot as it rotted, so he was too big to fit in the tomb. As the body was forced in, bits dropped off it!
- The smell was so bad the priests rushed through the funeral service … then ran!

But William the Conker wasn't the only monarch to have the bad burial blues…

# Foul funerals

1 **George IV** was so fat when he died, he barely fitted into his lead coffin. His bloated body began to expand and the lead coffin started to bulge. A hole was drilled in the lead to let out the gas, then it was sealed up again.

2 **George V**'s coffin was carried through the streets on a horse-drawn carriage. The crown stood on top of the coffin. During the bumpy journey the crown fell off and rolled into the gutter. 'A bad sign!' some people said. Sure enough, the next king, **Edward VIII**, gave up the throne after a few months. The crown was repaired – Edward never wore it.

3 Before Victoria's funeral most monarchs had been buried quietly at night. She demanded a big public funeral and they've been that way ever since.

Victoria was a very prim and proper queen –
but her subjects would have been shocked if
they'd known the truth about her grave secret.
Gossips said there had been funny goings-on
between old Vic and her servant, John Brown.
The queen's friends said 'Rubbish!' So, why
was she buried with John Brown's picture and
a lock of his hair clutched in her hand?

**4 William the Conqueror's** problems didn't
end with his messy funeral. Five hundred years
later vandals broke into his tomb and stole
everything except his thigh bone. Then, 200
years later, that was pinched too!

**5 William II** died in a hunting accident in
the New Forest. His body was dumped on a
cart and taken to Winchester Cathedral. It
dripped blood all the way. He was buried in the
ground under a cathedral tower. Seven years
later the tower fell down … William's ghost got
the blame!

And, talking about William II…

# William II (1087–1100) – Bad Billy

## Claim to fame
- A greedy, bad-tempered bully – at least that's what the monks who wrote the history said about him. But they *would* say that. He was nasty to them and their Church!
- Red hair and a redder face gave him the nickname Rufus – that's Latin for 'red'.
- Shot with an arrow while out hunting – probably murdered on the orders of his brother, Henry. (Another example of brotherly love, just like Ferrex and Porrux?)

## Cruel king
*The Anglo Saxon Chronicle* (an early history) said…

HE WAS VERY HARSH AND FIERCE IN HIS RULE OVER HIS REALM AND TOWARDS HIS FOLLOWERS AND TO ALL HIS NEIGHBOURS. HE WAS CONTINUALLY ANNOYING THIS NATION WITH PLUNDERING AND UNJUST TAXES. EVERYTHING THAT WAS HATEFUL TO GOD WAS THE DAILY PRACTICE IN THIS LAND DURING HIS REIGN, SO HE WAS HATED BY ALMOST ALL HIS PEOPLE

21

He wasn't even popular with his own servants …

**Funny Fact**
William was short, fat and ugly but he was proud of his appearance. His long, reddish-blond hair was parted in the middle and his clothes were always the latest fashion. To his servants, this sometimes made him a bit of a joke.

## Billy's sticky end

The big bad bully Billy decided to go hunting one day. The arrow-maker brought him six new arrows. He picked the best four and gave two to the knight, Walter Tirel. 'It's only right that the sharpest arrows should go to the sharpest shot!'

A letter arrived from the Abbot of Gloucester. It warned the king that there was danger if he left the safety of the castle. William ignored the warning and set off into the New Forest. He waited quietly by a deer track for an animal to come along. Walter Tirel stood at the other side of the track.

Sure enough a deer trotted down the path. Sharp-shot Tirel missed! But the arrow flew across the path and hit the king in the chest, killing him instantly. (It could have been worse ... Tirel could have hit the poor little deer!)

To this day, no one is sure if it was an accident (that was Tirel's story) or murder.

But think about it:

• If Tirel was such a good shot, how could he completely miss something as big as a deer?

> • He must have been either an awful shot...
>
> • Or a brilliant shot who actually hit the little target he was aiming at ... the king's heart!

23

**Fantastic fact**

William II died while hunting in the New Forest on 2 August 1100. The crown went to his enemy, and brother, **Henry I**. But, did you know that on 2 August 1100 Henry just happened to be out hunting ... *in the New Forest?* Coincidence?

William II reigned for 13 years. Was this unlucky 13 for William? Perhaps, but it seems that for British monarchs, an unluckier number has been the number *two*...

# TWO TOO UNLUCKY

Monarchs who were the *second* of their name have usually been unlucky!

**1 George II** died after having a fit and falling off the toilet.

HE'S LOOKING A LITTLE FLUSHED

**2 James II of Scotland** was attacking Roxburgh when one of his own cannons exploded and killed him.

**3 Charles II** died a long, slow, painful death ... killed by the clumsiness and stupidity of his own doctors!

**4 Henry II** blamed himself for the murder of his best friend, Thomas Becket, then had a miserable life fighting his own wife and rebellious sons.

**5 Edward II** ended his life in prison and was probably murdered there by a red-hot poker in the bowels.

**6 Richard II** was overthrown and probably starved to death in a cell.

**7 James II** of England was thrown off the throne for becoming a Catholic. He spent the last 11 years of his life in France where he was eventually buried. His daughter, **Mary II**, was glad to see the back of him and took his throne. When she arrived at his palace, she ran through the bedrooms and bounced on the beds for joy. But…

YIPEEE! I'M GOING TO BE QUEEN

Dear Mary,
Weather is fine, not sure about the Lord though. I'm still a Catholic so won't be returning to England, so the throne is all yours.
Wish you were here
love – James II (as was)

Princess Mary
England

**8 Mary II**, after snatching the throne from her old dad, died of smallpox having enjoyed the throne (and bounced on the palace beds) for just five years. She was 32 years old.

**9 Elizabeth II** has had so many popularity problems that she could well be the *last* monarch of Britain.

**10 William II** was probably murdered on the orders of his own brother, who went on to become Henry I…

# Henry I (1100–1135) – Henry the Horrible

## Claim to fame
- Afraid of being assassinated – he had nightmares about being killed. (Some historians reckon this was because he had a guilty conscience after paying Tirel to bump off brother Bill.)
- A strong king who ran the country well but could also be pretty vicious.
- Had the nickname 'Beauclerc', meaning 'good at reading and writing'.

## Cruel king
Henry's father, **William the Conqueror**, left Henry no land. But as William lay dying he left Henry £5,000 instead. As soon as his dad died, what did Henry do?
1 Hurried off to say a prayer.
2 Arranged the funeral.
3 Broke down and cried.
4 Rushed off to the treasury and had his fortune weighed out.

William II had that nasty accident with an arrow. What would horrible Henry do to Robert? He went to war with him and beat him. Henry was more merciful to brother Robert. He kept him in prison ... but only for 28 years.

### Quick quiz

Henry had a strong sense of loyalty. In 1090 a man made an oath to Henry's brother (and greatest enemy) Robert. The man broke that oath. How did Henry reward the man?

**1** Gave him his own weight in gold as a reward for betraying Robert.

**2** Sent the man back to Robert to be punished for his treachery.

**3** Pushed the man off the top of a tower as a punishment for lying.

**Foul fact**
Henry II died and his body was carried to the grave in an open coffin. His hated son, **Richard I,** arrived to meet the procession. As Richard leaned over the coffin, blood spurted from the nose of his dead father. 'His angry ghost doesn't want his son here!' the people muttered.

**Another foul fact**
Henry I was not a greedy eater and he didn't enjoy rich food as much as other royals. Yet he died of a fever after eating too maby lampreys – eels. His doctor had warned him not to.

# Suffering Stephen (1135-1154) and Miserable Matilda (1141)

## Claim to fame
• Stephen and Matilda fought each other for the English throne.

- Henry I had left his lands in France to his nephew, Stephen. He left the English throne to his daughter, Matilda.
- Greedy Stevie wanted both and invaded England. In the wars that followed, the biggest losers were the ordinary people.

## Cruel king and mean queen

Stephen and Matilda did the arguing, but the fighting and dying was done by the peasants. And while they were fighting, there was no one to care for the crops, so the families went hungry. No wonder a monk wrote...

I know not how to tell of all the cruelties they brought upon the people of this unhappy country. And so it lasted for nineteen years while Stephen was King, till the land was all undone and darkened with such deeds. Men said openly that Christ and his angels slept.

## Stevie's wonder

Stephen was fighting against John Marshall, leader of Matilda's forces. They agreed a truce. But Stephen wanted some guarantee that John wouldn't break the truce.

So John sent his six-year-old son, William, as a hostage. 'If I break the truce then you can kill my son!' John Marshall promised.

What did John Marshall do? He broke the truce without a second thought! After all, he had three other sons back at home!

'Your son shall hang!' Stephen threatened.

'Go ahead,' Marshall shrugged.

The happy little boy was led out to a nearby tree, not knowing what was planned.

He saw one of the guards with a fine new javelin and asked if he could play with it. Stephen was touched. But he had to hang the boy, otherwise Marshall would see Stephen as a weak man. His own men might even lose respect for him. These were cruel, hard times. What would you have done if you'd been Stephen? And, what did Stephen do?

1 Send the boy back to his father.
2 Hang the boy.
3 Keep young William.

*Answer:* 3 Stephen took the boy back to his own camp, spared his life and cared for him. William grew up to be a great soldier and repaid Stephen's family with many years of loyal service. But his sort of kindness did Stephen no good at all. His enemies saw it as a sign of weakness. They just fought him all the harder.

## Foul fact

**Queen Matilda** was not a popular woman in some parts of England. In 1141 she found herself trapped in the town of Devizes surrounded by enemy forces…

Matilda was dressed up in grave clothes like a corpse waiting to be buried. She was tied to a stretcher and the body was taken past the guards. Once the funeral party was well clear of Devizes the corpse sat up and laughed. 'Never get out alive, they said!'

A year later Matilda found herself trapped in Oxford. The tale of her escape from Oxford is one of the great stories of British monarchs. But is that story true? And how many of those other old tales are true?

# Tall tales

There are many incredible stories passed down the ages about British monarchs. Some of the stories were invented many years after the monarch died; the person writing the history wanted the old monarch to sound better (or worse) than they really were. For example, **Henry VII** had a history written about the king he had beaten in battle, **Richard III**. The history made Richard sound so bad that the people said, 'Wow! Aren't we glad to be rid of Richard!' They *forgot* to say, 'Hang on ... what right has Henry to kill the old king and take his crown?' Because the answer was, 'Not a lot!'

So, that's how stories about monarchs can actually be lies. Still, because they are good stories, historians and teachers remember them and repeat them until everyone believes they are *true*. Here are some famous 'stories'. Some are probably **true** – others are almost certainly **false**. But which are which?

**1 Queen Matilda** was trapped in Oxford Castle and surrounded by her enemy, Stephen. Just before the food ran out she was lowered from the castle on a rope and escaped over the snow-covered fields. She wasn't spotted because she wore a white cloak for camouflage.

**2 Richard I** spent 17 months as a prisoner in a castle. His faithful minstrel, Blondel, set off to search for him. He sat outside the walls of castles and sang Richard's favourite tune. Then, one day, he heard the king join in! He had found his lord.

I'VE GOT A LOVELY BUNCH OF COCONUTS...

...PLINKETY... PLONK...

BIG ONES, SMALL ONES SOME AS BIG AS YER 'EAD...

**3** The last word of **Charles I**, as he laid his head on the executioner's block, was 'Remember!'

**4 Victoria** was a miserable woman whose favourite saying was, 'We are not amused'.

**5 Richard III** died on the battlefield at Bosworth crying, 'A horse, a horse! My kingdom for a horse!' He didn't get one and was killed. His crown was found hanging on a thorn bush.

*Answers:*

**1 True** The cold journey nearly killed her but she made it eventually to the safety of Wallingford.

**2 False** The story was told by minstrels!

**3 False** As the executioner brushed Charles's hair to one side the king said, 'Wait for the sign'. These were really his last words – unless he said 'Ouch' as his head hit the ground, of course.

**4 False** There is no record of her ever saying that. In fact, in her diaries, she often wrote, 'I was very much amused'.

**5 False** William Shakespeare made up the words, 'My kingdom for a horse', in his play *Richard III*. The story about the crown is very unlikely.

Another famous rolay story is about the murder of the Archbishop of Canterbury in his cathedral. The story of Becket being hacked to death by a group of knights is certainly true. The Archbishop was Thomas Becket, and the king was **Henry II**...

# Henry II (1154–1189) – Hasty Henry

### Claim to fame
- Ruler of France and England.
- Was cursed with a wife (Eleanor) and sons (Richard, John and Henry) who went to war with him.
- Most famous for having Archbishop Thomas Becket murdered ... then spending the rest of his life regretting it.

### Cruel king
Thomas Becket was Henry's best mate. Henry made Tom Archbishop of Canterbury. They quarrelled and Henry complained that he wished he was rid of his old pal. Some knights thought he really meant it and gave Tom the chop. Henry was sorry – a bit late then, of course.

### Funny fact
Henry's queen, Eleanor, was a beautiful woman. A German poet once wrote...

36

*Were all the world mine*
*From the sea to the Rhine*
*I'd give all away*
*If the English Queen*
*Would be mine for a day.*

Not great poetry, but you get the idea. The poet forgot to mention that Eleanor turned very nasty when husband Henry upset her.

## Foul fact

Henry spent most of his later life fighting against Eleanor. She took sides in the 1173 rebellion against Henry when Henry found a new girlfriend, Rosamund Clifford. Henry had his wife locked in prison to stop her stirring up more trouble.

Henry was so protective of Rosamund that it was said he kept her in the middle of a maze ... and only *he* knew the way to the centre.

But one day his wife attached a thread to the heel of her husband's boot and was able to follow the thread to Rosamund's secret room. Queen Eleanor offered the young girl a poisoned drink. Rosamund sipped it and died.

37

What a story! Unfortunately, it's about as likely as Snow White being poisoned by the wicked queen. For Rosamund died in 1176 ... and Henry had Eleanor imprisoned in a tower from 1174 until 1189!

**Fantastic fact**
One day a knight was stupid enough to say something in praise of William the Lion, King of Scotland. William was Henry's deadliest enemy. Henry was so enraged, one historian said that he 'flung his cap from his head, pulled off his belt, threw off his cloak and clothes, grabbed the silk cover off the couch and started chewing pieces of straw.'

## The ghost of Thomas Becket
After the murder of Becket the knights went to an inn to rest and eat. If Thomas Becket's housekeeper had written a diary it might have looked like this...

Now I don't believe in ghosts. Archbishop Becket says believing in ghosts isn't Christian. So, I *didn't* believe in ghosts. Not until I saw what happened in the Archbishop's house tonight! Just imagine this...
   It's a bad night. Thunder rumbling in the sky. I'm just clearing the last of the supper dishes away. Then, suddenly, the door crashes open. I think at first it's the storm, but no. These four men walk in. I say 'men'. They are knights. I can tell. They have these dirty great swords hanging from their belts. Scare the life out of me!
   Anyway, one of them says, 'Prepare us a room for the night, my good woman.' My good woman, indeed!
   'This is not a tavern, you know,' I tell him.

That's when he pulls his sword out and waves it in my face. The great bully. Threatening a woman with a sword. I'm just going to tell him what to do with his sword when I notice the red stains on it. I can smell the blood. Fresh blood.

'I'm sure I don't know what Archbishop Becket would say,' I mutter.

The man puts his nose an inch from mine. 'The Archbishop won't say a word,' he growls. Then the others laugh as if he's said something funny. 'Anyway, we serve a greater man than Becket. We serve King Henry.'

They sit at the dining table, Archbishop Becket's table, and order me to fetch food. I'm not going to argue. They make me fetch the best wine and they drink it like water. All the time they're laughing and talking. Of course they're talking in French so I don't understand a word.

That thunder is getting louder and the storm is getting closer. Suddenly one jumps to his feet, says something and they all march out. A minute later they come back in carrying their saddles. 'If there's going to be a storm', one said, 'we don't want our saddles to get wet.' Then they throw the saddles on the table, Archbishop Becket's best dining table, and order more wine.

Then there's a loud clatter. I'm thinking, that storm must be right over our heads. But the knights have stopped laughing now. They're staring at the table. Then I realize it wasn't the storm that had made the noise. It was the table. It's moving.

That huge table takes four strong servants to move. Now it's moving itself. The oak feet are lifting up and rattling on the stone floor. Suddenly the rocking table gives one great heave and the knights' saddles fall to the floor.

The men just stare at them. The table has stopped moving. One man rubs his eyes as if they'd played tricks on him. He picks up his saddle and puts it back on the table. The others copy him. Then they stand and stare. The only sound in the house is the moaning of the wind in the chimney.

Then that rumble again. The table begins to tremble then it bucks and heaves like a wild horse. The saddles fly into the air and tumble to the floor.

The knight who'd threatened me turns to me now. 'Becket is angry,' he says. The man's face is pale as mutton fat.

'Archbishop Becket?' I said. 'Of course he'd be angry, seeing saddles on his table. But he can't throw them off if he's not here, can he?' I'm not scared of them any more. But I am getting mad. 'He's not a ghost, you know!'

The man's eyes widen till I can see the whites. His tongue hangs out as if it doesn't fit his mouth any more. He tries to say something, but can't. He just falls to his knees, puts his shaking hands together and prays. The others do the same.

The room lights up with a flash of lightning. The door rattles and opens slowly. The Archbishop's secretary is standing there. An old monk. His hands are stained as red as that knight's sword. He doesn't see the knights on their knees. I'm not even sure if he sees me. 'Archbishop Becket has been murdered,' he says.

I look at my lord Archbishop's table. I didn't believe in ghosts, until tonight.

'I know,' I say.

Of course, this story was told many years after the murder. It seems to show that the ghost of a murder victim cannot rest until the killers are brought to justice. There are many such stories of avenging ghosts. Are they true? It's for you to decide if you believe in ghosts or not.

The murder of Becket was one of the first supernatural tales told about a king. But there have been others…

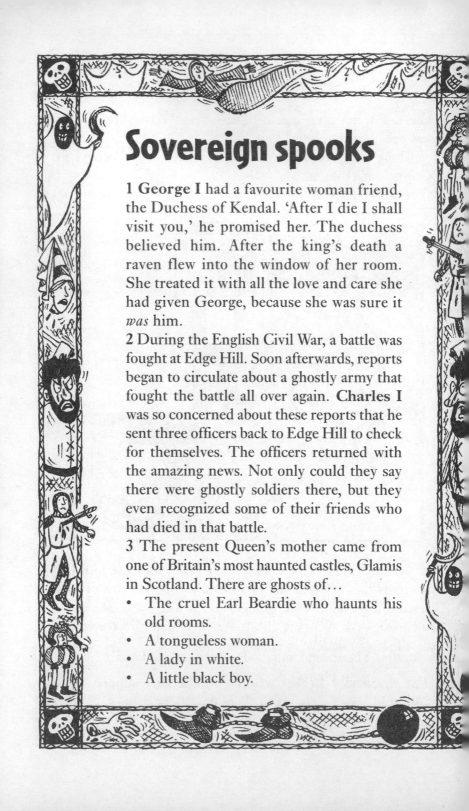

# Sovereign spooks

**1 George I** had a favourite woman friend, the Duchess of Kendal. 'After I die I shall visit you,' he promised her. The duchess believed him. After the king's death a raven flew into the window of her room. She treated it with all the love and care she had given George, because she was sure it *was* him.

**2** During the English Civil War, a battle was fought at Edge Hill. Soon afterwards, reports began to circulate about a ghostly army that fought the battle all over again. **Charles I** was so concerned about these reports that he sent three officers back to Edge Hill to check for themselves. The officers returned with the amazing news. Not only could they say there were ghostly soldiers there, but they even recognized some of their friends who had died in that battle.

**3** The present Queen's mother came from one of Britain's most haunted castles, Glamis in Scotland. There are ghosts of…

- The cruel Earl Beardie who haunts his old rooms.
- A tongueless woman.
- A lady in white.
- A little black boy.

- The Grey Lady said to be Lady Glamis who was buried alive. She has been seen by the Queen Mother herself.

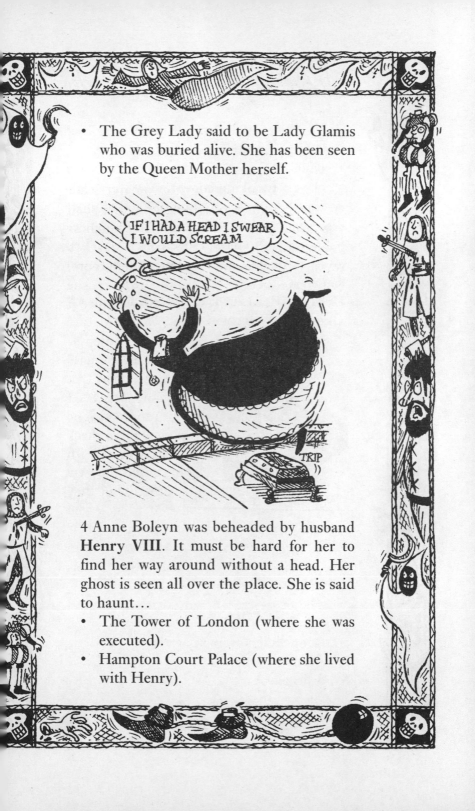

4 Anne Boleyn was beheaded by husband **Henry VIII**. It must be hard for her to find her way around without a head. Her ghost is seen all over the place. She is said to haunt…
- The Tower of London (where she was executed).
- Hampton Court Palace (where she lived with Henry).

- Blickling Hall in Norfolk (where she lived before her marriage).
- King's Manor in York (where she has a ghostly monk for company).

At least her ghost isn't lonely. Each of those places has several other ghosts in residence.

**5** If you want to meet a sovereign spook then go to Farnham Castle in Surrey. There you can meet…

**Henry VIII, Mary I, Elizabeth I, James I, George III, Victoria.**

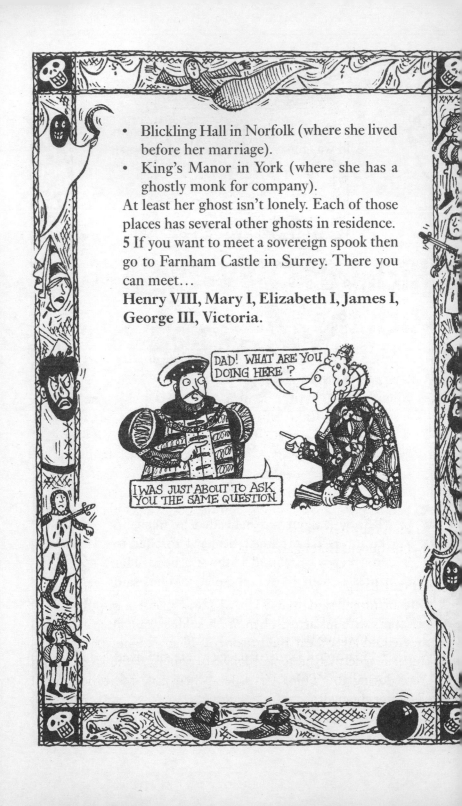

# Richard I (1189–1199) – Rich the Witch

## Claim to fame
- Spent so much time fighting in the Crusades he was hardly ever in England to rule. (Six months to be exact.) The Crusades were Christian armies setting out to recapture the Holy Land (Palestine) from the Muslims.
- On his way back from the Crusades he was captured by the Austrians and held to ransom. The English people had to pay a fortune to get him back. A high price for a king they never saw.
- His queen, Berengaria, *never* visited England.

## Cruel king
One historian said that Richard always kept a supply of prisoners with his army. Then, if his soldiers ran out of food, they could always eat the prisoners. That may not be true. But it *is* true that he took a lot of prisoners at the siege of Acre during the Third Crusade – then gave the order to slaughter them all.

## The tale of the silly servant

Richard was on his way home from the Third Crusade. He decided to take a short cut through Austria, even though the Austrian king was his enemy. (Emperor Henry VI of Austria said Richard had insulted his son.)

So a twitchy Richy had to travel in disguise. He was caught because he sent a stupid serving boy to an Austrian town market to buy food. The boy flashed gold coins around and even carried the king's glove on his belt. He was taken to the town castle for questioning…

**Foul fact**
**Richard I** was buried at Fontevraud, near his father ... but his heart was buried separately at Rouen.

**Funny fact**
Richard is usually seen as a bold, heroic warrior – 'Lionheart'. But, when the Austrians came to arrest him, he wasn't waiting ready to fight for his freedom. He was working in a kitchen, pretending to be a poor servant. A sort of Richard the Chickenheart. But Richard was caught out. How?
1 A serving girl was insulted by one of the searching soldiers. Richard drew his sword to defend her honour even though it cost him his freedom.
2 Richard was such a good servant that one of the other servants was jealous and betrayed the king.
3 Richard forgot to take off the royal ring he was wearing and that gave him away.

*Answer:* 3 The story goes that he forgot to take off his fat gold ring and that gave him away. He was arrested. But very similar stories have been told many times about *other* rich travelers in hiding. That bit is probably *not* true. What *is* true is that he was caught and imprisoned.

**4 Richard I** didn't have the luck of the Devil. That's surprising, because Richard is one monarch who's been linked to the Devil!

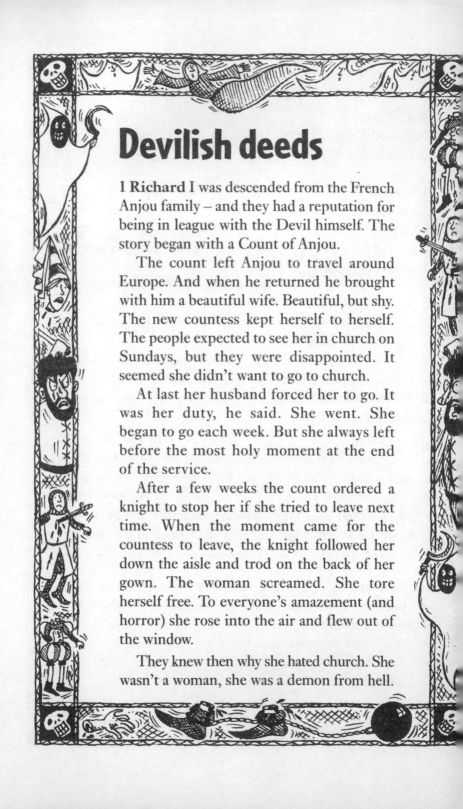

# Devilish deeds

**1 Richard** I was descended from the French Anjou family – and they had a reputation for being in league with the Devil himself. The story began with a Count of Anjou.

The count left Anjou to travel around Europe. And when he returned he brought with him a beautiful wife. Beautiful, but shy. The new countess kept herself to herself. The people expected to see her in church on Sundays, but they were disappointed. It seemed she didn't want to go to church.

At last her husband forced her to go. It was her duty, he said. She went. She began to go each week. But she always left before the most holy moment at the end of the service.

After a few weeks the count ordered a knight to stop her if she tried to leave next time. When the moment came for the countess to leave, the knight followed her down the aisle and trod on the back of her gown. The woman screamed. She tore herself free. To everyone's amazement (and horror) she rose into the air and flew out of the window.

They knew then why she hated church. She wasn't a woman, she was a demon from hell.

And her children were the children of the Devil. From that day onward, the Anjou family were said to have the Devil's blood in their veins!

**2 Henry IV's** wife, Joan of Navarre, was suspected of being a witch. Her priest accused her of plotting to kill her stepson, **Henry V**, by witchcraft – no one is sure why – and she was imprisoned without a trial for four years. She was released and lived quietly for another 15 years. Still, when she died, the *Chronicle of London* reported her death and added that 'all the lions in the Tower of London died in the same year'. The suggestion was that the lions were her helpers from hell. When she died they had no reason to live.

**3** Even kings believed in witchcraft. **James I** wrote a book on the subject after a witchcraft plot on his life…

**4 Henry VIII** had trouble with a witch who was also his wife. He accused Anne Boleyn of being a witch. That was one of the reasons he gave for having her executed. Daft Henry said he had *proof* that Anne was a witch. But what was it?

**a** He caught her flying on a broomstick.
**b** She had a black cat that talked to her.
**c** She had six fingers on her left hand.

*Answer:* **c** Anne was borne with six fingers on her left hand. *We* know that didn't make her a witch, of course. And it didn't stop Henry from marrying her. The sixth finger just became a useful excuse to get rid of a queen who had passed her sell-by date!

**5 Richard I's** brother, **John** – another Anjou, of course – was accused of being a different kind of devil. A werewolf, in fact! After he died, his body was heard to be moving underground – it couldn't rest under holy earth. So a group of monks dug him up and buried him outside the sacred ground!

Of course, **John** was one of those kings who upset the monks who wrote the histories. That was why they gave him such a bad name! John was said to be an awful king…

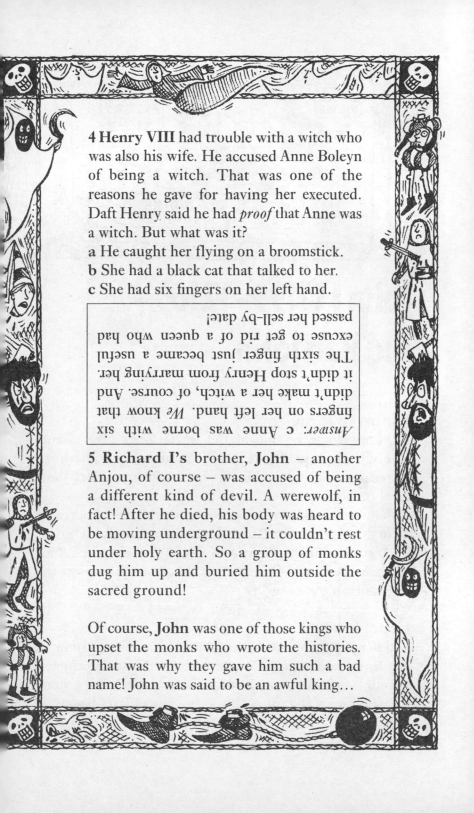

# John I (1199-1216) - Big Bad John

## Claim to fame

- Supposed to be one of the worst kings ever to rule England. Actually, he was a bit unlucky – the huge ransom England paid for Richard left the country short of money.
- John was forced to give power to the barons by agreeing to the Magna Carta (that's Latin for Great Charter).
- Argued with the Pope who closed the churches. This upset the monks … and it was the monks who wrote the history of John's reign.

## Cruel king

In 1203 John captured his troublesome nephew, Arthur. A gentleman and a knight would care for his noble prisoner, wouldn't he? John got drunk, killed Arthur, tied a stone round his body and threw the corpse in the River Seine.

**Funny fact**
Roger, a monk, wrote...

*In 1209 Geoffrey the Archdeacon of Norwich said that it wasn't safe for a priest to serve the king. King John was furious. Geoffrey was imprisoned in chains and given no food, so he died an agonizing death.*

Big Bad John up to his old tricks, you think? In 1225, Geoffrey the Archdeacon of Norwich became Bishop of Ely! We either have Geoffrey becoming bishop *16 years after he died* ... or we have Roger being a dodgy historian. Well ... even monks tell fibs.

**Fantastic fact**
**John** tried to cross the Wash – a stretch of water between Norfolk and Lincolnshire. The area is flooded when the tide is in but makes a good short cut when the tide is out. John began to cross, got the timing wrong and the tide came in.

He escaped with his life but lost his crown and chests of valuables. Treasure hunters today still hope to find them under the mud. This incident gave rise to…

**Ancient historical joke 1**

**Ancient historical joke 2**

But did King John *really* sign the Magna Carta at all? It's just one of the questions you can use to Test your teacher…

# Test your teacher

**True or false?**

**1 King John** did not sign the Magna Carta.

**2** The Battle of Hastings in 1066 was *not* fought at Hastings.

**3** A 'yard' was the distance from the thumb of **Henry I** to the tip of his nose.

**4 James I** was the first British monarch to take a trip in a submarine.

**5 Elizabeth I** had **Mary Queen of Scots** imprisoned for 19 years then executed, but the two women never met.

**6** Two hundred years after his death, King **Henry VIII's** finger bone was used as a knife handle.

**7 Old King Cole** was a British king.

**8** In the reign of **Henry II**, the king had the right to give a single woman in marriage and be paid for her.

**9 Queen Alexandra**, wife of **Edward VII**, walked with a limp. Fashionable ladies copied the limp. The walk became known as the Alexandra Glide.

**10 Queen Alexandra** nicknamed her daughter-in-law (wife of **George V**) 'Fat Mary'.

*Answer:*

**1 True** John couldn't read or write. He stamped the Magna Carta with the Royal Seal.

**2 True** The battle of Hastings was fought at Senlac Hill. Hastings was the nearest town.

**3 True.**

**4 True** A Dutch inventor called Drebbel made a wood and leather submarine in 1624. It used 12 rowers and James was a passenger when they tested it on the Thames.

**5 True** Although a film about them invented a meeting scene!

**6 True** Historians liked to dig up old skeletons of monarchs to find out more about them. They were then supposed to re-bury the skeleton. One historian kept Henry's finger bone as a souvenir.

**7 True** Coel the Splendid ruled Northern England and the Scottish Lowlands in the fifth century.

**8 True** The bride's 'price' was decided by her age, the land and livestock she owned and the number of children she had if she was a widow.

**9 True** She was also quite deaf. Fashionable ladies did not copy that handicap.

**10 True** But no one called Mary 'Fat' to her face – she'd probably have flattened them!

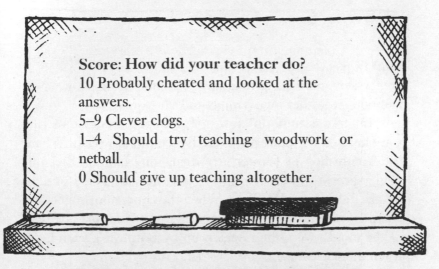

**Score: How did your teacher do?**
10 Probably cheated and looked at the answers.
5–9 Clever clogs.
1–4 Should try teaching woodwork or netball.
0 Should give up teaching altogether.

# Henry III (1216–1272) – Henry the Loser

## Claim to fame
- He ruled badly, taking huge taxes from the English people to fight hopeless foreign wars.
- He ruled for such a *long time* – 56 years.
- The Great Council began in Henry III's reign. It was the first parliament with people of the towns having some say in how England was run.

**Foul fact**

Henry sent his beautiful queen, Eleanor, to the Tower of London ... for her own protection!

Eleanor was unpopular with Londoners because of the way she used her power to make her own family rich. When the Archbishop of Canterbury died, for example, Eleanor made sure her uncle, Boniface, got the job. The London monks didn't want Boniface. When the chief monk objected, Boniface went to the monastery and thumped him. The rest of the monks were then beaten up by Boniface's friends to teach them a lesson.

The Londoners were furious and they besieged Eleanor in the Tower. Eleanor made a break for it down the River Thames. She was spotted and as her boat sailed under London Bridge, the people of London were ready for her. They pelted her with mud and rubbish. What did the lovely Eleanor do?

1 Pick up the rubbish and pelt it back.
2 Beg for mercy.
3 Die as the result of a direct hit from a cabbage.

*Answer:* 1

**Fantastic fact**
**Henry III** liked to hear priests say prayers. On his way to meet the French King, Louis, Henry stopped to hear prayers every time he met a priest on the road. This made him very late for his meeting. Next time Henry went to meet Louis, the French king had priests banned from the route!

## Jester's joke
Henry was often called 'Simple'. Yet a Jester said…

**Whose zoo?**
Whose zoo was the first zoo? **Henry III's**, that's whose zoo. Henry was given three leopards as a present by Emperor Frederick II. Henry kept them in the Tower of London. People were allowed to come and visit the animals. This was so popular that Henry began to collect other unusual animals.

In 1251 the King of Norway sent Henry a polar bear – complete with its keeper. It (the bear!) was often seen on the end of a long lead, fishing in the River Thames for salmon. These were the first in a line of curious palace pets…

# Palace pets

**1 Henry I** had a collection of animals at Woodstock in Oxfordshire as early as 1115. They included lions, leopards, lynxes and an African porcupine. But this wasn't a true zoo because it was a private collection for the king's amusement.

**2 Richard II** was given a camel by the people of London. But to stop the queen from getting the hump they gave her a pelican as a Christmas present.

**3 George V** had a pet parrot. He liked to take it down to breakfast with him. The parrot wandered across the table, helping itself to breakfast. But, what goes in must come out and the bird often messed on the table. This annoyed the queen. So George was in the habit of moving the mustard pot over the bird dropping to hide it.

**4 James I** was obsessed with lions – the symbol on his Scottish crown. He bred them and had an exercise ground built in the moat of the Tower of London where they lived. A popular 'sport' in James's day was bear-baiting. A chained bear was attacked by dogs and they fought to the death (or deaths). James decided it would be interesting to have the bear attacked by a lion. He put the two in a ring together. What happened?

a The lion killed the bear.
b The bear killed the lion.
c The two wouldn't fight.

*Answer:* c The miserable lion slunk away and didn't want to fight.

**5 Henry VIII** had hunting hounds who ate scraps that the king threw from the table. But after he died and was lying in his coffin, some attendants reported that the hounds were looking lovingly at Henry's body … and licking their lips!

# Edward I (1272–1307) – Big Ed

### Claim to fame

- Respected as a strong king and a good soldier.
- Beat the Welsh and gave them his baby son to be their prince – the Prince of Wales.
- He went on to bash the Scots and pinched their coronation stone – the Stone of Scone. It's still in Westminster Abbey and has been used for every coronation to this day. Ed beat the Scots in battle so many times he became known as the 'Hammer of the Scots'.

## Cruel king

Edward was accused of being a bit of a cheat in battle. He captured some banners from one of the enemy barons and flew them over his own army. So, of course, the other enemy barons didn't attack him. When he was close enough he showed his true colours – and attacked them. Their leader, Simon de Montfort, was captured and beheaded.

## Funny fact

The roads of England weren't safe for travellers. Outlaws and highwaymen lurked in the forests ready to jump out and rob you. **Edward I** was fed up with this so he rode out to meet a leading outlaw and challenged him to a fight. They agreed that, if Edward won, then the highwayman and his band would go away and never bother travellers again. What happened?

1 Big Ed won the fight and made the road safe.

2 The outlaw refused the challenge, robbed Ed and rode off laughing.

3 The outlaw won the fight but gave up robbing out of respect for the gallant king.

*Answer:* 1 The outlaw had been a knight so it was a fair fight which Big Ed won.

## Foul fact

In 1303, Edward's Crown Jewels were stolen from Westminster Abbey. Richard de Podlicote spent 98 days tunnelling under the walls to reach the treasury. He had a bit of help ... 48 of the monks from the Abbey.

The theft succeeded and Richard sold off the precious

cups and plates to the London goldsmiths who displayed them in their windows! Richard was arrested as a result. He was hanged ... the monks went free!

Richard's skin was stretched across the treasury door as a warning to anyone else who fancied nicking Ed's gold. Yuk!

## Fantastic facts
Big Ed was said to be the luckiest monarch of England.

1 As a boy he was playing chess in a castle. Suddenly, and for no good reason, he jumped to his feet and walked away from the chess table. Moments later, a huge stone crashed down from the roof on to the chair where young Ed had been sitting. Lucky Ed was nearly a flat 'ead.

2 In 1272 Edward was in Palestine. A visitor arrived and said he had to speak to the English king. They showed him into Edward's tent. 'Your Majesty,' the man said. 'My business is so secret I must speak to you alone!' Edward dismissed his guards. As soon as they were alone the man drew a poisoned knife and stabbed Ed in the arm. Ed kicked at the killer, knocked him down with a stool and grabbed at the knife. In the struggle the king received another wound on the forehead. The man was overpowered but Ed was seriously ill. He even made his will. But his luck held and he survived. (One poem says, 'Eleanor, his gentle wife, sucked out his wound and saved his life.' Another story says she made such a fuss that the doctor sent her from the room and cured the king without her help. That's more likely.)

3 In Paris, a ball of lightning flashed down from the sky. It flew past Ed's shoulder and missed him.

Lucky for him? Yes. It hit two of the king's servants. Not so lucky for them. They died.

4 In one battle a stone from a huge mechanical catapult was hurled at Ed. It missed him. Lucky for him? Yes. Not so lucky for the horse he was riding. The stone hit the animal and flattened it.

Big Ed also battered the Welsh a lot and made his son, Little Ed, the first Prince of Wales. The knighting of Little Ed was just one of the curious tales about princes…

# Potty history of princes

In 1306, Edward's son was to be knighted. To make it a special occasion another 300 young men were to be knighted at the same time. Have you ever tried to get 300 men round one altar in a church? Don't. In 1306 many were injured – two died.

SWIPE

OH DEAR! IT'S A GOOD JOB THERE'S ANOTHER 298 TO PRACTISE ON

**1** There have been 20 Princes of Wales, but only two 'Princes of Whales'. The first (because he was so fat) was Prince George who became **George IV**. The second is the present **Prince Charles** who is the only prince to have ridden on the back of a killer whale.

**2** Many kings hated their princely sons. **George I** hated his son, Prince George (later **George II**). For years the two only met at christenings – and usually ended up having arguments there. After one squabble, George I tried to have his son arrested for attempted murder.

**3 George II** went on to hate his own son, **Prince Frederick**, just as much. George II said…

OUR SON IS THE GREATEST ASS. THE GREATEST LIAR AND THE GREATEST BEAST IN THE WHOLE WORLD AND I WISH HE WAS OUT OF IT

At least Frederick's sister had some kinder words for the ugly little pop-eyed prince. She said, 'He is a sick-making beast who cares for nobody but his sick-making self.' Charming!

**4 Edward VII**'s son, **Prince Albert Victor**, was so fond of dressing up in the latest fashions that he was given the nickname 'Prince of Collars and Cuffs'.

**5 George V**'s son, **Prince Harry**, never grew up. In old age his hobby was watching children's television. One evening his cousin, the King of Norway, came to visit the prince. Harry kept him waiting till he'd finished watching the latest episode of *Popeye*.

The son of **Edward I** grew up to be nothing at all like his father…

# Edward II (1307–1327) – Thick Ed

### Claim to fame
- Being hammered by the Scots … not to mention by his father, the barons and, finally, his wife.
- Wasn't a keen soldier and lost the famous Battle of Bannockburn to the Scots. He preferred swimming and dressing up.
- Came to a very nasty end…

### Mean queen
Edward II's wife, Isabella, was one of the most evil of the Brit queens ever to rule. She wanted rid of the king (Edward II) so her son, **Edward III**, could take over the throne.

But she didn't want any signs of violence to show that hubby Edward II had been murdered. First she got her boyfriend, Roger Mortimer, to raise an army and attack King Edward. When Mortimer had captured the king, Isabella ordered Edward to be thrown in jail.

Underneath the jail the corpses of dead prisoners were left to rot. She hoped Ed would die from an infection. He didn't. He was then left to starve. He didn't. Isabella then sent a message to the jailers. It seemed a harmless enough message. In fact it was a code. It meant, 'Kill him!'

First they smothered the king with cushions, then pushed a hot poker into his bowels from underneath so the entry wound was not too easy to spot. That certainly did the trick. Isabella gave Ed a lovely funeral and even went along herself.

**Funny facts ... and figures**

Match the numbers to the facts...

| NUMBER | FACT |
|---|---|
| 6 | a. QUEEN ISABELLA WAS THE DAUGHTER OF ... MONARCHS. |
| 2 | b. ISABELLA WAS THE SISTER OF ANOTHER .... MONARCHS. |
| 18 | c. EDWARD WAS ENGAGED TO ISABELLA WHEN SHE WAS ... YEARS OLD. |
| 13 | d. ED LOST HIS MOTHER WHEN HE WAS .... YEARS OLD. |
| 3 | e. ED WAS HIS PARENTS' CHILD NUMBER .... BUT THE ONLY BOY TO SURVIVE. |
| 4 | f. £ .... THOUSAND WAS HOW MUCH ISABELLA'S FATHER GAVE EDWARD TO MARRY HER. BUT THE WAY THE MARRIAGE TURNED OUT .... MILLION WOULDN'T HAVE BEEN ENOUGH. |

ANSWERS: a2. b3 c4 d6 e13 f18

**Foul fact**

Isabella hated her husband, Edward, and had him murdered, yet she was buried with his heart clutched to her chest – a sign of true love. Eleanor, a poet, called Isabella 'The she-wolf of France'.

That was just one of many nicknames monarchs have had...

# Nutty nicknames

Can you match the nickname to the owner?

| MONARCH | CLUE | NICKNAME |
|---------|------|----------|
| 1. GEOFFREY (HUSBAND OF MATILDA) | – NICE FELLER? | a. BLEARIE (BLOODSHOT EYES) |
| 2. EDITH (WIFE OF HAROLD) | – BIG SWALLOW? | b. SOFT-SWORD |
| 3. JAMES II OF SCOTLAND | – HOT STUFF? | c. SWAN NECK |
| 4. GEORGE IV | – BIT OF A NINNY? | d. SILLY |
| 5. ROBERT II OF SCOTLAND | – SIGHT FOR SORE EYES? | e. HAREFOOT |
| 6. JOHN I | – FIGHTING FLOP? | f. THE FIERCE |
| 7. HAROLD | – RUN RABBIT RUN? | g. THE HANDSOME |
| 8. WILLIAM IV | – WILLY THE WALLY? | h. FIERY FACE |
| 9. CHARLES II | – SORRY, WRONG NUMBER? | i. CHARLES THE THIRD |
| 10. ALEXANDER OF SCOTLAND | – TEMPER, TEMPER | j. PRINNY |

*Answer:*

**1 g** Geoffrey the Handsome (because he was handsome, I suppose).

**2 c** Edith Swan Neck (because of her pale, long neck).

**3 h** James II Fiery Face (because of a red birthmark on his face).

**4 j** George IV Prinny (short for Prince of Wales – which he was for many years).

**5 a** Robert II Blearie.

**6 b** John I Soft-sword (because he lost a lot of battles).

**7 e** Harold Harefoot (because he was a fast runner).

**8 d** William IV Silly (because he was a Silly Billy).

**9 i** Charles II Charles the Third. (Charles had a girlfriend called Nell. She'd had two boyfriends before the king, both called Charles. So, to her, he was the third Charles – Charles the Second was Charles the Third, get it?)

**10 f** Alexander the Fierce (because he was fierce, you might think).

Other people in the royal courts were given nicknames too. **George** I had *two* girlfriends (the greedy man). He brought them with him from Germany, and the British people hated them both. They made a curious couple. One was tall and thin, one was dumpy and fat. They were nicknamed 'The Maypole' and 'The Elephant and Castle' – no prizes for guessing which was which!

Princes had their nicknames too. **Edward III's** son, also called Edward, was known as the 'Black Prince'. He took his nickname from the dark armour he wore into battle...

EDWARD III
RULER OF FRANCE, SET SQUARE OF ENGLAND

# Edward III (1327–1377) – Slob Ed

## Claim to fame

- Fought against the Scots *and* the French ... but not at the same time.
- Called himself the king of France even though he wasn't. The war with France went on a long time. So long that King Ed died after reigning 50 years and the war was still going on. In fact, it became the Hundred Years war.

_your name_

# IDIOT'S EXAM PAPER

1. WRITE YOUR NAME AT THE TOP OF THE PAPER

2. ANSWER THE QUESTION: HOW LONG DID THE HUNDRED YEARS WAR LAST?

A : 100 YEARS

B : 116 YEARS

C : 99 YEARS

*Answer:* **b** The war started in 1337 and didn't end until 1453.

- Ruled during the terrible plagues of 1348–50, the Black Death, and was father to the Black Prince.

Edward revived the idea of a knights' Round Table like the legendary Arthur. But it was the English archers with their longbows that really won the battles.

## Mean queen

Edward had trouble with greedy women in his life.

- His queen, Philippa, wanted to borrow money from Germany. So she promised the moneylenders Edward's Crown Jewels ... it cost the king 30,000 packs of English wool to get the jewels back.
- At the end of his life he had a girlfriend called Alice Perrers. She watched old Ed die ... then pinched the rings off his dead hands and disappeared with them. She lived comfortably on the proceeds until her death 23 years later.

## Foul fact

Many English kings were messy eaters ... but **Edward III** was a very messy reader. His teacher complained that he ruined his books by:

- Letting his nose dribble over the pages.
- Marking his place with thick stalks of straw so the book split when it was closed.
- Eating fruit and cheese or drinking while reading and allowing it to slop on the pages.
- The disgusting youth also had filthy finger nails.

But Edward III wasn't the only mucky monarch...

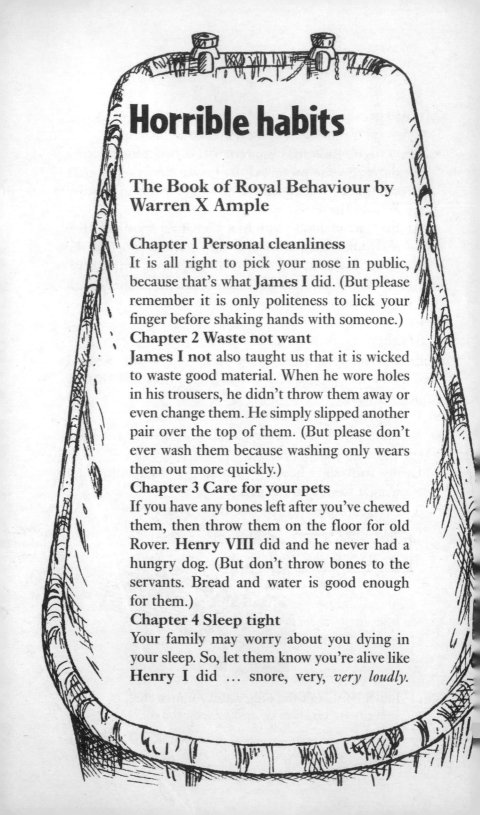

# Horrible habits

## The Book of Royal Behaviour by Warren X Ample

### Chapter 1 Personal cleanliness
It is all right to pick your nose in public, because that's what **James I** did. (But please remember it is only politeness to lick your finger before shaking hands with someone.)

### Chapter 2 Waste not want
**James I not** also taught us that it is wicked to waste good material. When he wore holes in his trousers, he didn't throw them away or even change them. He simply slipped another pair over the top of them. (But please don't ever wash them because washing only wears them out more quickly.)

### Chapter 3 Care for your pets
If you have any bones left after you've chewed them, then throw them on the floor for old Rover. **Henry VIII** did and he never had a hungry dog. (But don't throw bones to the servants. Bread and water is good enough for them.)

### Chapter 4 Sleep tight
Your family may worry about you dying in your sleep. So, let them know you're alive like **Henry I** did ... snore, very, *very loudly*.

(The others in the palace won't get a wink of sleep, of course, but the lower classes don't need as much sleep as a monarch. Anyway, they should be awake to guard you.)

**Chapter 5 Have a good spit**

When in public it is quite all right to spit. Spit often and spit large quantities. **William IV** did this. Some people said he was not a gentleman. But he had been in the navy a long time and, like other sailors, was used to spitting into the sea (where the fish probably objected … but why should he worry, he wasn't the 'Prince of Whales', was he?)

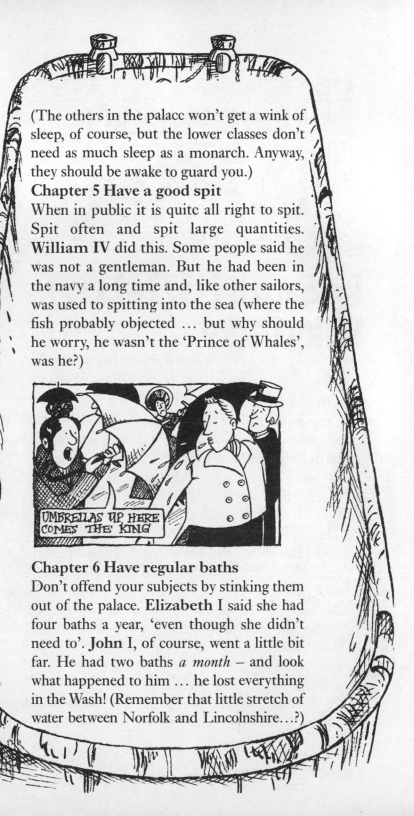

**Chapter 6 Have regular baths**

Don't offend your subjects by stinking them out of the palace. **Elizabeth** I said she had four baths a year, 'even though she didn't need to'. **John** I, of course, went a little bit far. He had two baths *a month* – and look what happened to him … he lost everything in the Wash! (Remember that little stretch of water between Norfolk and Lincolnshire…?)

# Richard II (1377–1399) – Sicky Dicky

## Claim to fame

- Came to the throne when he was just ten years old. The coronation was so exhausting he collapsed and had to be carried out on the shoulders of his attendants.
- At 14, he fought against the peasants, led by Wat Tyler, who revolted against a tax they hated called the *Poll Tax*. Ricky talked the peasants out of the rebellion, promised them a lot but gave them nothing.
- He had no children of his own so his reign was filled with squabbles about who would be king after he died. He made himself very unpopular by trying to rule without the help of Parliament. He was such a rotten ruler that, in the end, his cousin **Henry IV** took the throne from him. Richard starved to death in prison.

## Foul fact

When **Richard II** lost the throne, he was imprisoned in Pontefract Castle. He not only lost the throne – he also seemed to lose the will to live. He almost certainly starved himself to death.

Many people began muttering that Richard had been murdered, so his body was paraded through the streets of London in an open coffin and people were allowed to see the corpse for themselves.

After his death there was another rumour. Some people said that Richard II had been born without a skin. They claimed he was brought up wearing the skin of goats.

## Funny fact
**Richard II** was really upset when his queen, Anne, died at Sheen Palace. In fact, he was so annoyed that he had the palace knocked down.

Still, he decided to marry again. He was 29 years old when he married his second queen, Isabella of France, in 1396. There was a bit of an age difference between them – 22 years, in fact. Isabella was just seven years old.

When the new girl-queen arrived in London, people crowded on to the streets to see her. Nine people were killed in the crush on London Bridge.

**Fantastic fact**

**Richard II** is supposed to have invented the handkerchief. Unfortunately, he invented it too late for his grandfather, **Edward III**, whose teacher complained his nose could do with a good blow.

He wasn't the only monarch to start a trend…

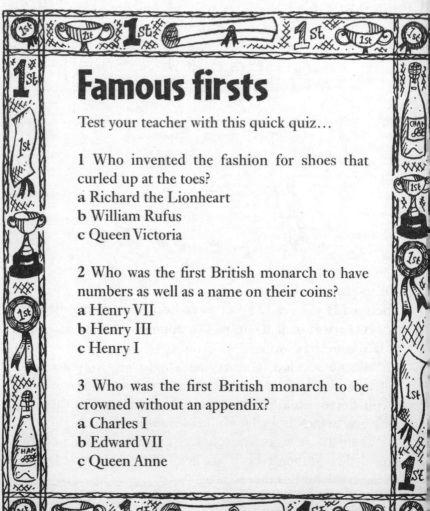

# Famous firsts

Test your teacher with this quick quiz…

1 Who invented the fashion for shoes that curled up at the toes?
a Richard the Lionheart
b William Rufus
c Queen Victoria

2 Who was the first British monarch to have numbers as well as a name on their coins?
a Henry VII
b Henry III
c Henry I

3 Who was the first British monarch to be crowned without an appendix?
a Charles I
b Edward VII
c Queen Anne

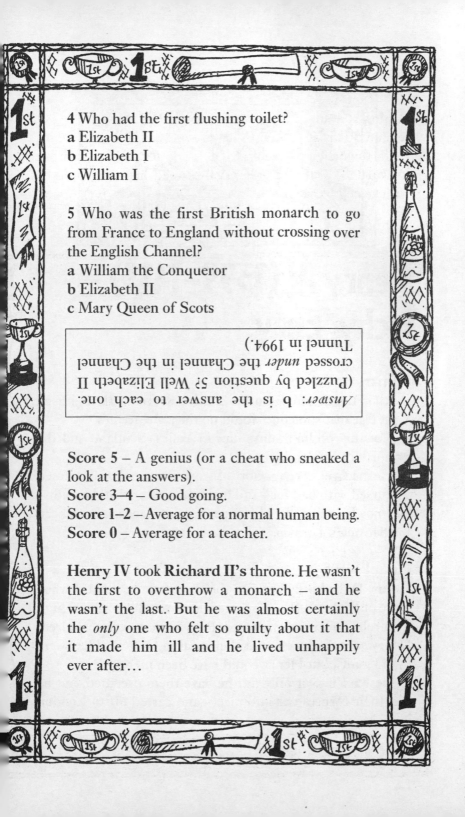

**4** Who had the first flushing toilet?
**a** Elizabeth II
**b** Elizabeth I
**c** William I

**5** Who was the first British monarch to go from France to England without crossing over the English Channel?
**a** William the Conqueror
**b** Elizabeth II
**c** Mary Queen of Scots

*Answer:* **b** is the answer to each one. (Puzzled by question 5? Well Elizabeth II crossed *under* the Channel in the Channel Tunnel in 1994.)

**Score 5** – A genius (or a cheat who sneaked a look at the answers).
**Score 3–4** – Good going.
**Score 1–2** – Average for a normal human being.
**Score 0** – Average for a teacher.

**Henry IV** took **Richard II's** throne. He wasn't the first to overthrow a monarch – and he wasn't the last. But he was almost certainly the *only* one who felt so guilty about it that it made him ill and he lived unhappily ever after…

# Henry IV (1399–1413) – Itchy 'Enry

## Claim to fame

- Took the throne from his cousin, **Richard II**, and lived in fear that someone would do the same to him.
- Lots of revolts against him in Wales, Scotland and the north of England.
- He had the Archbishop of York executed and seemed cursed with bad luck and bad health after that. He didn't enjoy his reign. As Shakespeare said, 'Uneasy lies a head that wears a crown.'

## Cruel king

**Henry IV** had only been on the throne three months when some of **Richard II's** supporters led a rebellion against him. The rebellion was a failure and its leaders were captured. Henry sat in judgement at their trial in Oxford. They were found guilty, but Henry could have been merciful.

He wasn't. Not only did he have them executed, but he had their corpses cut into pieces and carted off to London in sacks.

While Richard II lived there was always the chance of rebellions in his support. Shortly after this first rebellion, Richard died. Coincidence?

Henry also refused to tell Richard's young queen, Isabella, what had happened to her husband. He simply took Isabella's jewels from her and divided them among his own children.

**Fantastic fact**
**Henry IV** had taken the throne from the rightful king, **Richard II**, and this was said to be a sin. Stories went around that there were evil signs all around the kingdom. They included...

• A boy born with one eye in the middle of his forehead.
• A calf born with two tails.
• Eggs which, when cooked and opened, showed the face of a man with white hair.

Henry himself seemed to suffer from this 'curse' – his hair was filled with lice, his spotty skin itched and his eyes were dry, red and sore. He was a mess of a monarch!

**Foul fact**

Henry's son, Prince Hal, couldn't wait to get his hands on the crown. 'Your father is dead,' the doctors told him. 'You are King Henry the Fifth.'

Young Hal rushed to the sick room and looked at the crown by the side of his father's bed. The old king's face was covered. The young man reached out and grasped the crown and took it away.

Then there came a soft moan from the bed. The doctors raised the cloth from the face. Old Henry opened his eyes. 'The crown,' he whispered. 'Where is the crown?'

'Your son has taken it, sire.'

'Send for him!'

The prince returned to find his father clinging on to life. 'Sorry, father. They told me you were dead. I took the crown because I am your oldest son, the next king'.

Old Henry sighed. 'I had no right to wear that crown, so why should you?' he asked.

'You held the crown by the right of your sword. I shall do the same,' the prince said.

The old king nodded. 'Do whatever you think best. I leave it all in the hands of God ... and hope that he will have mercy on me.'

He said no more and died shortly after.

**Henry IV** had so many lice in his hair it was said that his hair wouldn't grow! Henry was said to suffer from leprosy; a punishment for his having the Archbishop of York executed. Being a monarch didn't save him or other kings and queens of Britain from illnesses and the cruel curses of...

# Dreadful doctors

**1 William III** was fed powdered crabs' eyes by his doctors. It was meant to cure his fever. It didn't. He died.

**2 Queen Anne's** doctors tried…
- Letting blood out of her body.
- Red–hot irons to blister the skin.
- Medicines to make her vomit.
- Covering her feet in garlic.
- Shaving her head completely bare. Anne died.

**3 Charles I** didn't really expect to be king. His older brother, Henry, was the first in line to the throne. But Henry fell ill with typhus. Doctors suggested a remedy of pigeons pecking at the bottom of his feet! Henry died.

**4 Henry VI** had a mental illness. His doctors tried to cure him by giving him pills and potions that didn't work. They then shaved off the king's hair and probably cut a hole in his skull in an attempt to let the 'badness' out. (Don't try this on your teacher no matter how crazy you think they are.) Henry survived … but died a few years later when somebody made a much bigger hole in his skull with a sword. That cured his madness once and for all.

**5** When **George VI** was young, the doctors feared his legs were not growing straight. So every night the prince's legs were strapped into wooden splints. He didn't get much sleep, but the cure seemed to work.

But **Henry V** must have had some faith in doctors. He took ten surgeons with him when he went off to fight the Battle of Agincourt in France…

*Drill hole in skull, Thereafter take headache pills three times a day*

SIGNATURE:

DATE: 25.6.1407

# Henry V (1413–1422) – Hooray Henry

### Claim to fame

- The Shakespeare play shows him as a wild young man who calmed down and became a popular king. That is probably all made up by the playwright.
- Went to war against the French and devastated them at the Battle of Agincourt.
- Great soldier – awful haircut.

### Cruel king

At the battle of Agincourt, the English took a lot of French prisoners. They were sent to the back of the English army. Then there was a fresh French attack. Henry was worried that the prisoners would join in and attack him from the back. He ordered that all the French prisoners should be put to death.

### Famous last words

Henry died at the age of 35. He died of dysentry while fighting in France. He had always wanted to fight in the Crusades in Palestine. He said, 'I want to live long enough to rebuild Jerusalem's walls.' Then he died.

**Funny fact**

The French king decided to make fun of Henry. He sent the young English king a present. Tennis balls. The message was, 'You'd be better off playing tennis than trying to make war against France'. Henry crossed the Channel and his small army beat the large French army.

**Henry** V was not the only king who enjoyed a game of tennis...

# Good sports

**1 George VI** played tennis at Wimbledon … and won a trophy.

**2** Cruel **Henry VIII** went off for a game of tennis while his wife, Anne Boleyn, was being beheaded.

**3 Mary Queen of Scots** had a billiard-table to while away the long years she spent in prison. She also enjoyed a game of golf, just like **Charles I**. While he was a prisoner in Newcastle he was allowed out into the fields outside the town to play a game of 'gof'. Both played golf – both had their heads chopped off. Is there some connection?

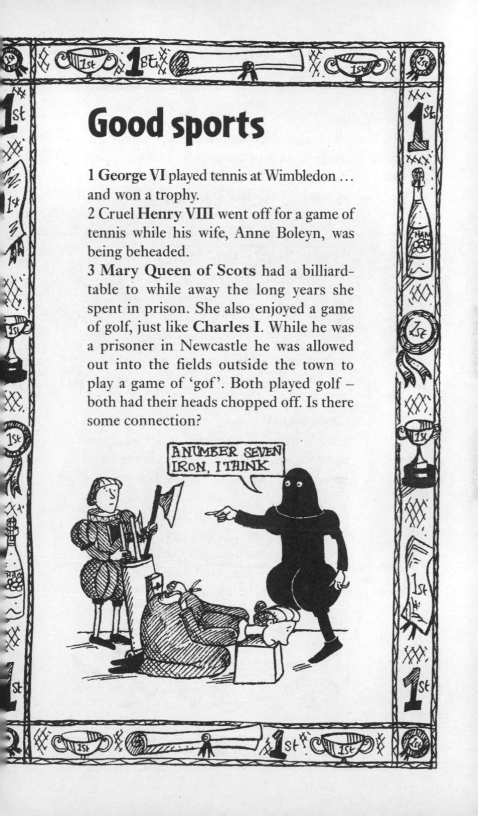

A NUMBER SEVEN IRON, I THINK

**4 George V** enjoyed shooting game-birds like grouse and pheasants. Once, he and his hunting friends killed 10,000 birds in a season. They even managed 1,000 in a single day. But ... one day, George V was walking in his garden when he found a dying bird. What did he do?

**a** Burst into tears.

**b** Wrung its neck.

**c** Cooked the bird and ate it.

> *Answer:* **a** George wept over a single bird yet cheerfully massacred thousands.

**5 Edward IV** passed a law in 1477 which made it illegal to play cricket. This law was not in force in 1715. Maybe it ought to have been, because British history was changed by a game of cricket. Britain has never had a King Fred ... but it *should* have. The son of **George II, Prince Frederick**, would have become king when his father died. But Fred died first. He was hit by a cricket ball and died in 1715.

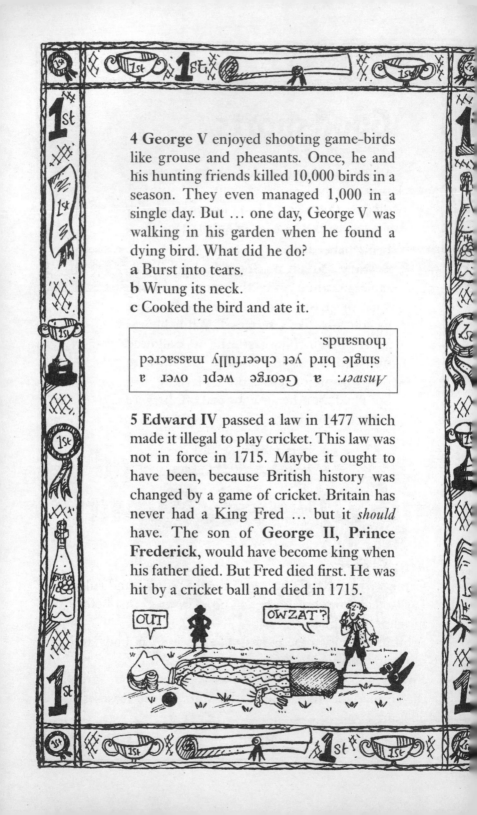

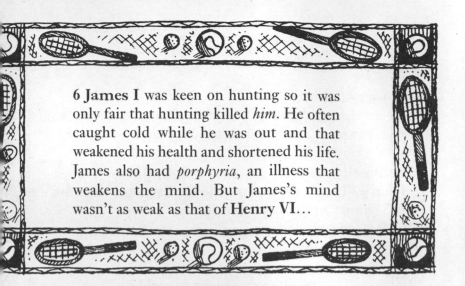

**6 James I** was keen on hunting so it was only fair that hunting killed *him*. He often caught cold while he was out and that weakened his health and shortened his life. James also had *porphyria*, an illness that weakens the mind. But James's mind wasn't as weak as that of **Henry VI**...

# Henry VI (1422–1461 and 1470–71) – Henry Halfwit

## Claim to fame
- Came to the throne at the age of eight months and ruled Parliament from his mother's knee. Crowned just before his eighth birthday.
- A bit of a wimp, to be honest. He was weak in body and mind and claimed to hear angels singing.
- Strong nobles decided this was their chance to grab the throne and they fought the Wars of the Roses for 30 years.

**Flowery fact**
Henry was murdered at the Tower of London in 1471. Every year, roses and lilies are laid at the spot in his memory.

**Fantastic fact**
**Henry VI** had a mental breakdown that lasted from August 1453 until Christmas 1454. Henry...
- Sat still and silent for hours like a statue.
- Lost his memory.
- Didn't recognize anyone.
- Found it difficult to move without help.
- Didn't know his wife had given birth to their son. When he recovered his memory, Queen Margaret was able to tell him he had a new son, the baby Prince Edward.

Henry's mental illness was as bad as that of his grandfather, **Charles VI** of France. Charles began to believe he was made of glass and could not be touched. He fitted iron rods into his clothes in case he fell over and shattered.

**Foul fact**

People of the Middle Ages were believers in the Devil and they were sure that the Devil had human helpers on earth. The helpers were called witches! When Henry VI became mad in 1453, a group of Bristol merchants got hold of one of the king's cloaks and cast a spell over it.

**Funny fact**

Henry had the job of opening Parliament. He was taken to Westminster but sat and cried all the way through the ceremony. He did have an excuse. He was only three years old at the time.

**Henry VI** wasn't the only monarch to burst into tears…

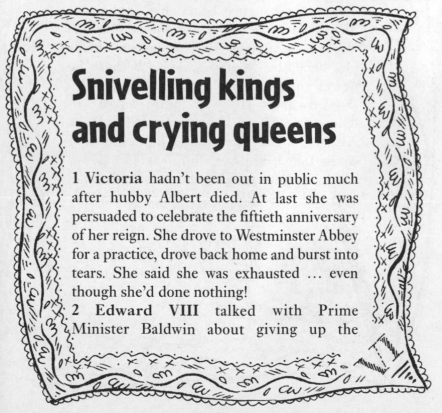

# Snivelling kings and crying queens

1 **Victoria** hadn't been out in public much after hubby Albert died. At last she was persuaded to celebrate the fiftieth anniversary of her reign. She drove to Westminster Abbey for a practice, drove back home and burst into tears. She said she was exhausted … even though she'd done nothing!

2 **Edward VIII** talked with Prime Minister Baldwin about giving up the

throne (abdicating). They agreed that Ed had to go. As he left, Baldwin said, 'Whatever happens, my missus and I wish you happiness.' Ed burst into tears.

3 While he was a young king in Scotland, **James I** was kidnapped and forced to sign a document sacking his 'protectors'. The sixteen-year-old king wept floods of tears as he signed. His kidnappers were not impressed. 'It's better that bairns should weep than bearded men'.

4 **William the Conqueror** was one of England's toughest kings – he believed that mutilating or blinding criminals was even better than hanging them. This was because the villains stayed around to remind others to behave themselves. But, as he lay on his deathbed, he wept constantly because he feared going to hell.

5 **Edward II** was imprisoned in Gloucestershire in 1327 and treated badly by his jailers. They made him a mock crown of straw and shaved him with the cold water of the River Severn. Edward took it on the chin and said…

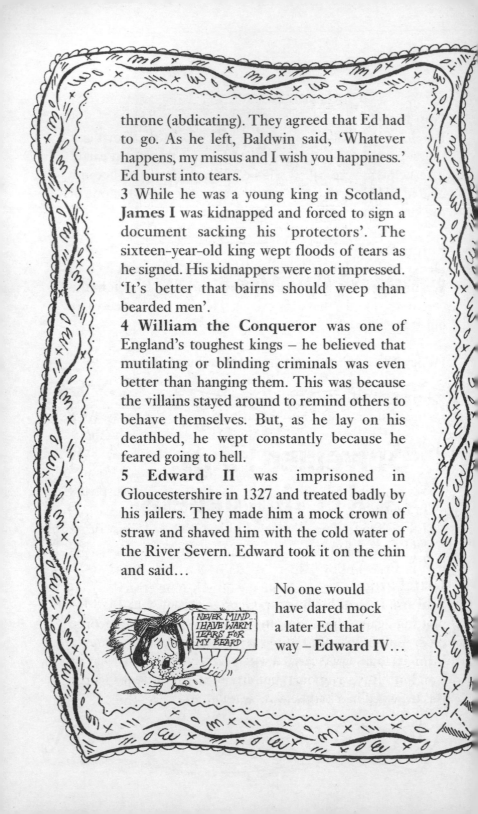

NEVER MIND… I HAVE WARM TEARS FOR MY BEARD

No one would have dared mock a later Ed that way – **Edward IV**…

# Edward IV (1461 –1483) – Hard Ed

## Claim to fame
- Invaded France. The French paid him to go away. As a result he was the first king since **Henry II** to die without owing money.
- A good soldier so, if he missed the fighting in France, he had plenty to do in the Wars of the Roses back in England.
- Loved food, wine, dancing and hunting, but most of all he loved ... himself.

## Cruel king
**Edward IV** had his brother, George, executed in 1478 for plotting against him. But no one is very sure *how* George died. A chronicle of the time says, 'the execution, whatever form it took, was carried out secretly in the Tower of London'. But a rumour went around London that George was drowned in a barrel of sweet wine.

The question is, would Edward really spoil a good barrel of wine when a quick blow with the sword would do just as well? One story even said he was drowned in a bath.

**Foul fact**
**Edward IV** had some luck in winning the Wars of the Roses. For a start his enemies helped ... by killing each other.

While **Edward IV's** enemies were killing each other, Ed was killing his own friends – and relatives. It's fairly certain that Ed's brother, George, Duke of Clarence, died in the Tower of London on Edward's instruction. The fate of Edward's son, little **Edward V**, is not so certain…

# Edward V (1483) – eleven-week Ed

## Claim to fame

- **Edward IV** died and left his brother, **Richard III**, to look after his thirteen-year-old son, **Edward V**, until the boy was old enough to rule for himself. Richard 'looked after' Edward V by locking him in the Tower of London with his brother, little Richard.
- After 11 weeks, the Bishop of Bath declared that Ed's father had never been properly married to his mother, so Ed couldn't be king. Richard III took over.
- What happened to Ed after that is a 500-year-old mystery. Was Ed murdered in the Tower by Richard III? Or did the new king move Ed to Yorkshire and look after him until **Henry VII** came to the throne? And so did Henry then murder them? No one really knows.

**Foul fact**
Did you know … **Edward V** was king for such a short time that no one had a chance to paint his portrait.

## Cruel king

The historian, Thomas More, wrote the story of the Princes in the Tower several years after their disappearance. He said they were...

- Murdered on the orders of uncle **Richard III**.
- Buried 'at the foot of the stairs, deep in the ground under a heap of stones'.
- Later dug up and re-buried by a priest.

But Thomas More was a historian for **Henry VII**, who was trying to prove how good he was by showing how *evil* Richard III was.

Some bones *were* found under the foundations of the White Tower stairs in the Tower of London in 1674. Workmen were demolishing the staircase when they came across two skeletons. (You'll notice this does not agree with Thomas More's story of their being buried 'at the foot of the stairs' and later moved.)

The skeletons were examined by a doctor and a dentist in 1933. They said they were the remains of two children aged ten and twelve ... just the ages the princes would have been if they had died in the reign of their uncle Richard. But the bones just might have been there since the year 1100 and could have belonged to some other poor children.

There is certainly no proof that Richard was responsible for their deaths. Many books have been written about the Princes in the Tower. Some prove that Richard murdered them ... some prove that Richard couldn't possibly have murdered them. The truth is that nobody knows.

Let's make no bones about it, the Princes in the Tower isn't the only grisly tale involving British monarchs...

# Any old bones

1 At the Battle of Agincourt in 1415 the Earl of Oxford and the Duke of York were killed. **Henry V** didn't want to bury the two nobles in France. On the other hand there'd been a lot of dysentery in the English army and they didn't want to risk more illness by carrying two mouldering bodies back to England. So they boiled the bodies till the flesh came off the bones. The skeletons were packed in a box and carted off home. When Henry himself died the same thing happened to his body.

2 The remains of **Henry VI** (who died in 1471) were dug up in 1911. The hair on the skull was seen to be covered in blood.

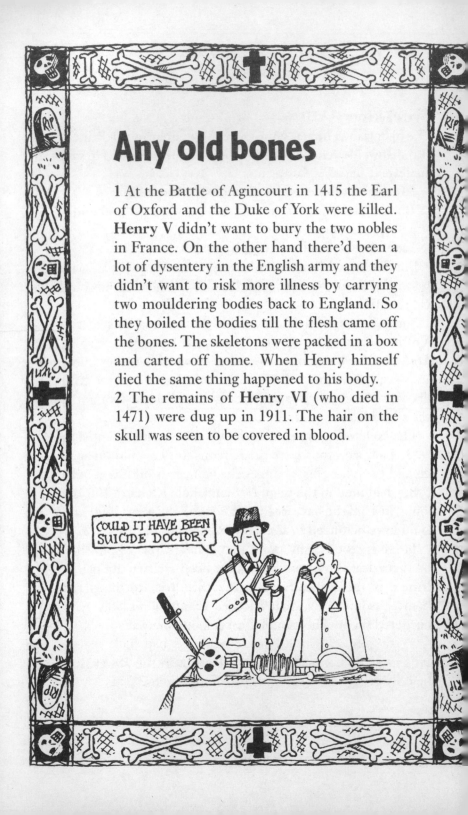

COULD IT HAVE BEEN SUICIDE DOCTOR?

**3 Henry VIII** was a Protestant ... but his daughter **Mary** I was a Catholic. There is a story that when Mary came to the throne she had Henry's bones dug up. Because he was one of those wicked Protestants, she had his body burned.

**4** Catherine, wife of **Henry V**, was mummified after her death in 1437. Later her body was dug up and kept above ground for over 300 years. For a few pence, inquisitive people could view the corpse in a chest. The writer, Samuel Pepys, saw the mummy in 1669 when he wrote the following gruesome account in his diary...

*I had the upper part of her body in my hands and I did kiss her mouth. I did kiss a queen on this my birthday. Thirty-six years old that I did first kiss a queen.*

**5 Henry IV** died in Westminster Abbey in 1413 but asked to be buried in Canterbury. Roads were very bad in the fifteenth century so his body was taken on a boat, down the Thames and round the Kent coast.

A story went about that a fierce storm sprang up during the journey. The superstitious crew believed it was because the unlucky king was carrying his bad luck with him ... so they threw the king's body over the side and popped another body in before the funeral at Canterbury. A silly story, but ... the king's tomb was opened in 1832. The archaeologists found...

- The inner coffin was a completely different shape from the outer one – had the swapped body come in its own coffin?
- The space between them was filled with straw – was this to stop the old coffin rattling and giving the game away?
- There were no royal riches buried with the body – had the sailors taken the chance to pinch them?
- On the inner coffin was a simple cross made of twigs bound together – was that the best the coffin-robbers could do for the dead king's soul?

**Richard III's** bones had an even worse time...

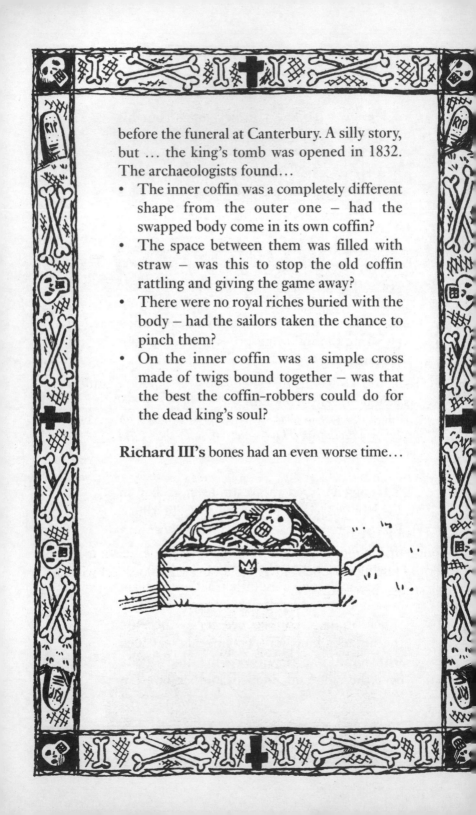

# Richard III (1483–1485) – Tricky Dicky

## Claim to fame
- Took the crown from his nephew **Edward V** and is suspected of murdering him.
- Lost it at the Battle of Bosworth Field where Richard was killed, to **Henry VII**.
- He is either loved or hated by many people. Some say he was a heroic soldier and a strong leader – some say he was a villain who was ugly and twisted. Nobody can agree…

## Cruel king
One story about **Richard III** concerns his execution of Lord Hastings. Richard invented an excuse to quarrel with Hastings then said…

I WILL NOT EAT MY SUPPER TONIGHT UNTIL YOUR HEAD IS OFF YOUR SHOULDERS

Men-at-arms rushed in and dragged Hastings out. They didn't have a block handy so they borrowed a piece of wood from a carpenter who'd been doing some repairs. Richard enjoyed his supper. Hastings didn't.

**Foul fact**
**Richard III** was the last English king to die on the battlefield. By wearing his crown he made himself the clear target for the soldiers of his enemy, Henry Tudor. Richard charged straight for Henry and cut down the Tudor flag – not to mention the man holding the flag. But Richard's horse was brought down and he was chopped to bits by Henry's soldiers.

**Fantastic fact**
Richard was buried in an unmarked grave. His stone coffin was paid for by Henry Tudor who went on to become **Henry VII**. There is a story that the coffin became a horse trough for many years. Later, it was said to have been broken up to make steps for a pub cellar. But what really happened to old Rick's final resting place? He was found just over 500 years later beneath a car park in Leicester.

**Funny fact**
**Richard III**'s life is depicted in a play by William Shakespeare. Richard is shown as an ugly hunchback with an evil history. Some people think this is terribly unfair. They say Richard was a strong but fair ruler and Shakespeare had it all wrong. They formed The Richard III Society. He is probably the only king of England to have his own fan club.

**False fact**
The night before the fatal Battle of Bosworth Field, **Richard III** was haunted by dreams of demons. 'A sign that England will be ruined,' he said. 'Whoever wins will destroy the supporters of the loser.'

*Wrong*! Henry's victory actually ended the Wars of the Roses and brought *peace*. The great victim of Bosworth Field was not England, but Richard.

There's a very strange story that started with Richard's defeat…

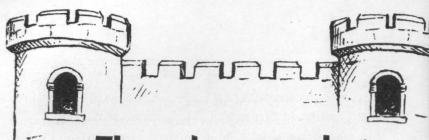

# The palace prophet

Robert Nixon wasn't too bright. He was just 16 years old in 1483 and only fit to follow the plough.

Robert didn't speak much and, when he did, he didn't talk a lot of sense.

One day he stopped ploughing and suddenly called out, 'Now Richard! Now Henry! Oh ... badly done, Richard ... well done, Henry! Henry's the winner!'

His fellow workers shook their heads sadly. 'Daft as a brush,' they muttered. Until...

The next day the sensational news arrived. At the very moment daft Robert was calling, the Battle of Bosworth Field was being won and lost. And, just as the ploughboy had dreamed, it was won by Henry Tudor and lost by **Richard III**.

Now Robert Nixon was no longer the village idiot – he was a great prophet.

News of the ploughboy prophet reached the ears of the new king, Henry Tudor, now **Henry VII**. The king sent for young Robert.

At that very moment Robert saw it. 'The king will send for me,' he whispered.

'That's good. He'll make you rich, lad.'
But Robert turned pale. He began to shake.
'No, no, no,' he moaned. 'He'll starve me
to death.'

Within two days the king's command
arrived. The miserable ploughboy had to
obey. He said goodbye to the villagers as if
he knew it was for the last time, and set off
for London.

Henry was no fool. He tested the powers
of the ploughboy. 'Can you find a hidden
jewel?' he demanded. Robert found it.
Robert passed every test Henry Tudor could
think of.

'You're a wonder, boy,' he said. 'You will
come and live at court. You will have
comfort for the rest of your life … what?
Are you not happy?'

'You'll starve me to death,' the prophet
said softly.

Henry gave a laugh, 'That's one prophecy that won't come true. Here! Marshal! Take Robert to the kitchens and see he gets all he ever needs to eat.'

And Robert lived a good life with the best food, and even seemed to forget the threat of his own prophecy.

One day, Henry had to leave London. He left his Marshal in charge of the palace … and in charge of Robert Nixon. Then the Marshal too was called away. The man worried about the boy. He worried for his safety. The other servants could be spiteful in their jealousy of Robert. So, to make quite sure the boy was protected, the Marshal locked him in a tower room.

The Marshal had problems once he left London. Problems that kept him away. Problems that made him forget the imprisoned prophet.

The Marshal held the only key to the tower room. By the time he returned to the palace Robert Nixon was dead.

He had starved to death … just as he said he would.

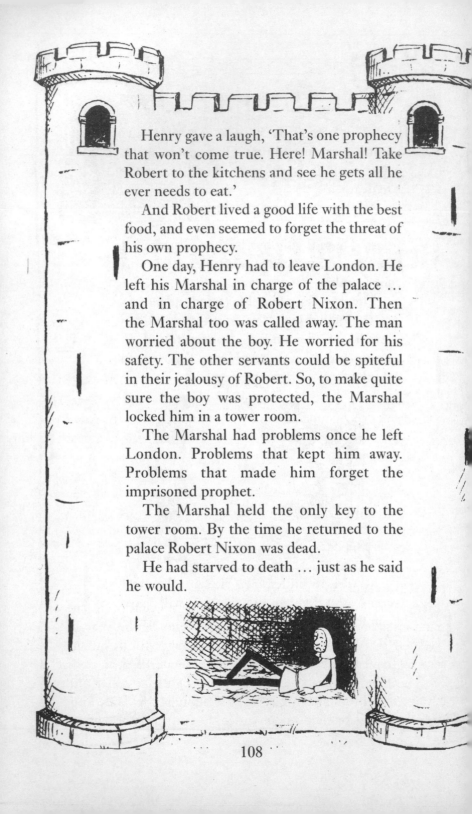

108

# Henry VII (1485-1509) - The Tight-fisted Tudor

### Claim to fame

- After taking the crown from **Richard III, Henry VII** made sure he kept it. He married Richard's niece, Elizabeth – a smart move which put his former enemies on his side. England was united after the long Wars of the Roses.
- During Henry's reign, two young men came forward and each claimed to be one of the Princes in the Tower, and the rightful king. Henry defeated both rebellions and kept a tight grip on the crown.
- He also kept a tight grip on his money.

### Cruel king

Henry VII was poorly. And what made it worse were the rumours that he'd be dead before the end of the year. It seemed that an astrologer had read Henry's future in the stars. He was going around predicting Henry's death.

The king was angry. He sent for the fortune-teller and they seemed to be having a friendly enough chat. The king asked if it was really possible to see the future in the stars.

'Why, certainly,' the fortune-teller said boldly.

'Very well,' King Henry smiled and showed his small, black teeth. 'Tell me where you will be this coming Christmas holiday.'

'Well ... er ... I'm not too sure,' the man mumbled, not so bold this time. He turned pale.

The king leaned forward with a cruel glint in his eye. 'You see,' he said softly, 'I am a better fortune-teller than you. For I do know where you'll be this Christmas. You'll be in the Tower of London!' He turned and called to the guards behind the throne. 'Take this foolish man away!'

'Where to, your highness?'

'Why, to the Tower, of course.'

## Fantastic fact

There were at least ten people with a better claim to the throne of England than Henry Tudor. One of them was his own mother. No wonder he was so worried about a rebellion from another hopeful ruler.

## Furry fact

Henry VII had a pet monkey. There is a story that the monkey got into Henry's writing room and tore up his diaries. Since the diaries had notes about the people in Henry's court, it is possible that one of them let the monkey in – and had a good laugh.

## Sad fact

Henry VII grew old before his time (unlike many monarchs, whose lives were chopped short) and his doctors could do nothing for him.

# Henry VIII (1509–1547) – Henry Ate

## Claim to fame

- Got rid of the Catholic Church in England and made himself head of the new Church. That gave him the chance to divorce his first wife and also to pinch the riches of the Catholic Church.
- He built the first modern navy.
- He liked hunting, eating, riding, eating, archery, eating, music, eating … and getting his own way. Anyone who annoyed him tended to get the chop – even a good friend like Thomas More.

## Cruel king

Henry was famous for his cruelty. Some of his worst acts were…

1 Henry held a party. He dressed in bright yellow, had a thanksgiving service at church followed by feasting, jousting and dancing. What was he celebrating? The death of his first wife, Catherine of Aragon.

2 Henry insisted on wife number two, Anne Boleyn, going through a long, difficult coronation ceremony even though she was expecting a baby. Not only was she tired – she also needed to go to the loo quite often. She couldn't leave the coronation ceremony to do this, so two ladies-in-waiting sat *under* her table with a potty.

3 When Anne gave birth to a daughter Henry was upset. He wanted a son. He showed Anne how annoyed he was by refusing to go to the christening.

4 When he grew tired of Anne Boleyn, he had her accused of having other boyfriends. Her only real crime was that she couldn't produce a baby boy who could be the next Tudor king of England.

5 As soon as Henry heard the cannon fire that signalled Anne's death, he set off for the house of his next love, Jane Seymour. They were engaged the next day. Jane was his favourite wife – maybe because she gave him a sickly son, Edward, before she died.

6 He agreed to marry his fourth wife, Anne of Cleves, after seeing a painting of her. She looked attractive. When he met her he realized she was not so pretty – so he divorced her.

7 Henry married Catherine Howard when she was just 19 but decided to have her executed when he heard she'd had other boyfriends before she married him. The young woman ran to him, screaming for mercy, begging to be allowed to live. He ignored her pathetic pleas and sent her to her death. Within a week of the execution he was celebrating with a feast again.

8 Wife number six was due to marry Henry's brother-in-law, Thomas Seymour. The greedy old king took her for himself instead, not caring about how poor Thomas felt. Never

mind – Henry died less than four years later and Catherine Parr finally married Thomas.

**9** Henry wasn't satisfied with having his enemies' heads lopped off. After Thomas More's head was cut off, it was boiled then stuck on a pole over London Bridge. This was to show people what happened to anyone who messed with Henry. More's daughter was allowed to have it for burial after three months.

**10** It's easy to see why Thomas More was happy to die rather than live under such a rotten ruler. He thanked Henry for ridding him of 'the miseries of this wretched world.' More's famous last words as he climbed the scaffold were…

## Foul fact

Anne Boleyn had an eating disorder. She would very often eat a meal ... then be sick before she could leave the table. Her ladies-in-waiting became used to this and would hold up a sheet in front of her while she vomited into a bowl. Of course, Henry was supposed to have written the song, *Greensleeves*. Was it inspired by Anne's sickness? And could Henry have added a verse like...

*Alas, my love, you are looking bad;*
*Perhaps it's the mouldy old peas you had.*
*I used to love the white dress, it is sad,*
*Because since you've been sick it's got green sleeves!*

## Fantastic fact

Anne Boleyn's head was cut off quickly and cleanly while she prayed. So quickly, in fact, that it is said her lips moved after her head was severed.

## Funny fact

Henry had six wives. But not many people know that wife number six (Catherine Parr) had *four* husbands of her own including Henry.

## Mean queen

Everyone knows about Henry's bloodthirsty nature. But they forget about his wives' nasty little habits. For example, Catherine of Aragon was left in charge of England while Henry went over to France. While he was away, Catherine's armies fought the Scottish king, **James IV**, and beat him at the battle of Flodden Field. Just to prove what a clever girl she was, Cathy sent Henry the blood-stained coat of the dead Scottish king.

## Not-so-mean queen

Rumour said that wife number two (Anne Boleyn) poisoned wife number one (Catherine of Aragon). But people *would* say that ... Catherine was popular – Anne wasn't. In fact, when Anne went to her coronation in a fine procession, people crowded the London streets to see her – but *no one* cheered. The doctor's report on Catherine's body describes something more like cancer. So, it's 'Not guilty, Anne.'

*Did you know...?*

**Henry VIII** wrote a book. He wrote about how wonderful the Catholic Church was – so the Pope gave Henry the title, 'Defender of the Faith' ... then the Pope refused to allow him to divorce his first wife. Henry left the Catholic Church, but he kept the title. All British monarchs since have called themselves 'Defender of the Faith'. In the same book, Henry argued that marriage should be for ever!

Henry was not the only monarch to write a book...

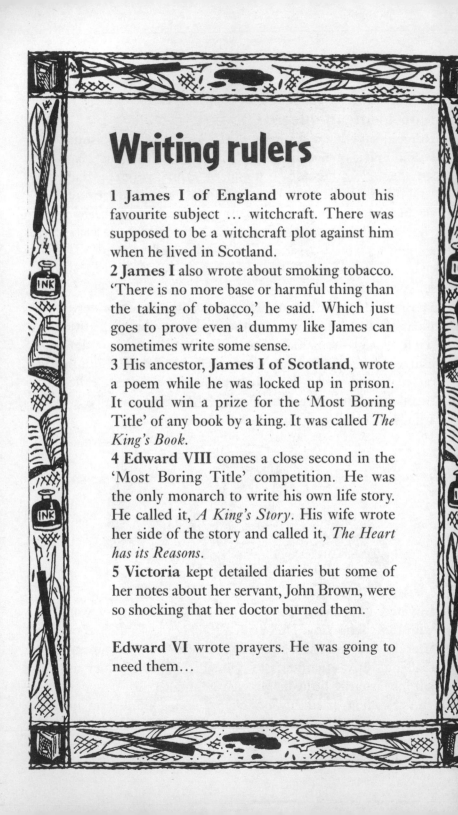

# Writing rulers

1 **James I of England** wrote about his favourite subject ... witchcraft. There was supposed to be a witchcraft plot against him when he lived in Scotland.

2 **James I** also wrote about smoking tobacco. 'There is no more base or harmful thing than the taking of tobacco,' he said. Which just goes to prove even a dummy like James can sometimes write some sense.

3 His ancestor, **James I of Scotland**, wrote a poem while he was locked up in prison. It could win a prize for the 'Most Boring Title' of any book by a king. It was called *The King's Book*.

4 **Edward VIII** comes a close second in the 'Most Boring Title' competition. He was the only monarch to write his own life story. He called it, *A King's Story*. His wife wrote her side of the story and called it, *The Heart has its Reasons*.

5 **Victoria** kept detailed diaries but some of her notes about her servant, John Brown, were so shocking that her doctor burned them.

**Edward VI** wrote prayers. He was going to need them...

# Edward VI (1547–1553) – Weak Ed

## Claim to fame

- Aged nine when his father, **Henry VIII** died and Ed came to the throne.
- Brought in the English Prayer Book, which caused a spot or two of bother.
- The last thing he wanted was his Catholic sister, Mary, to get her bum on the throne. But he did the wrong thing ... he carelessly died at the age of 15.

## Cruel king

**Edward VI's** uncle, Lord Seymour, wanted a quiet word with the young king. He decided to creep to Eddie's room after dark. Seymour took a loaded pistol and slipped through the king's private garden. But Eddie had bolted his door and left his favourite little dog on guard outside.

As Seymour tried the door latch, the dog jumped up and started yapping. Seymour panicked. He shot the dog!

117

Of course, the shot brought the guards running. Seymour was arrested and taken to the Tower. Edward might have forgiven the man his sneaky trip … he couldn't forgive the killing of his dog. Uncle Seymour got the chop.

**Fascinating fact**
Edward's nurse was called Mistress Sibell Penn. She died in 1562 from smallpox, nine years after nursing little Ed through his death. She was buried in old Hampton Church near Hampton Court. But when the church was pulled down in 1829 her remains were scattered. Then strange noises were heard at Hampton Court from the rooms where she'd lived. They sounded like the whirring of a spinning wheel. When the wall was taken down, guess what was found hidden there? Yes, a spinning wheel.

Since then her tall, grey, hooded figure has been seen wandering round, arms raised and pleading, before she disappears through a wall. At Hampton Court she has lots of ghostly royal company, including little Ed's mum and dad.

**Foul fact**
Edward died of a lung disease, tuberculosis, at the age of 15. But he also had one or two other nasty symptoms…

EDWARD VI
ERUPTIONS CAME
OUT OVER HIS SKIN
HIS HAIR FELL
OFF AND THEN
HIS NAILS AND
AFTERWARDS THE
JOINTS OF HIS
TOES AND
FINGERS

118

**Funny fact**

Edward was a good student. He had to be. His teacher, Dr Cox, used to beat him if he did badly in his lessons. Edward got his own back by setting up lots of schools (so other boys could go there and get beaten).

Even the royals had a hard time as children…

# ƝURSERY ƝASTIES

1 When **Charles I's** wife, Henrietta, gave birth to a son she was a bit disappointed. He was a strong, healthy child but his mother had to admit…

HE IS SO UGLY THAT I AM ASHAMED OF HIM

The ugly baby grew up to be **Charles II**.

2 Anne's son, **Prince William**, was always weak and sickly. He often lost his balance and was frightened of climbing stairs without help. But if his father, George, caught anyone helping the Prince then poor William was beaten. Anne just stood by and let it happen.

3 When he was a child, **Charles II** had to suffer some pretty nasty medicines. These included potions of rhubarb and senna. So he suffered both sickness and diarrhoea.

4 An English lady once visited **George II** in Germany. She found George's wife, **Queen Caroline**, whipping one of their children. 'Ah,' George said. 'You English have no good manners because you are not brought up properly.' The whipping was George's idea of bringing children up 'properly'.

5 **George V** said…

# Mary I (1553–1558) – Flaminq Mary

## Claim to fame

- Married the King of Spain, then got England drawn into Spain's battles with France. Her unpopular marriage caused an English rebellion led by Thomas Wyatt. Wyatt lost the first battle and was executed.
- Fanatical Catholic – had Protestants burned at the stake if they didn't change back to her religion.
- A sickly and unhappy woman who went down in history as 'Bloody Mary', though she wasn't cruel in herself … just trying to do what she thought right.

## Mean queen

As young **Edward VI** lay dying he did a silly thing. He wanted to stop Mary taking the throne. So he was persuaded to name Lady Jane Grey as the next monarch.

But Jane was no older than Eddie and she had very little support compared to Mary. Eddie practically gave Jane Grey a death sentence. Jane was thrown off the throne after just nine days and Mary sentenced her to be beheaded, along with her young husband, Lord Guildford Dudley.

But the execution was particularly cruel. Instead of getting it over with quickly, poor Jane had to watch her husband being taken off to execution first. She then had to watch as his dead body was brought back on a cart – with his head wrapped in a cloth.

After that horror she was taken to her own death. Her sad little ghost has been seen wandering the Bloody Tower in the Tower of London.

**Foul fact**
**Mary I** hated Protestants … and Protestants hated Mary. Some Protestants sneaked into Mary's room at Whitehall and left behind a dead dog. Its head had been shaved, like the head of a Catholic priest. Its ears had been clipped and there was a noose around its neck. This was a hint as to what would happen to Mary's Catholic priests. Mary was furious and swore revenge. She got it.

Anyone who refused to convert to Catholicism died a slow and painful death, by burning at the stake. Mary had 283 Church of England supporters burned, including an Archbishop of Canterbury. One dead–dog joke cost a lot of lives.

Mary I was responsible for many cruel deaths but her sister, **Elizabeth I**, managed to equal her. The difference was that Mary killed as many in her five years as Liz did in 45!

## Cruel king
Mary married Philip, the king of Spain. But Philip was a pretty awful choice. He…

- Left Mary soon after their marriage. He returned to Spain and broke Mary's heart.
- Wanted to be sure he kept the throne of England if sickly Mary ever died – so he flirted with Mary's sister (who became **Elizabeth I**), while Mary was still alive.
- He tried to grab the throne of England after Mary died with what he called his 'Unbeatable Armada' – it was beaten.
- Was far more cruel to non-Catholics in Spain than Mary ever was to Protestants in England.

But Philip wasn't the only monarch involved in murdering…

# Murder and monarchs

1 Isn't this strange? In 1100 a man called Tirel was accused of murdering **William II**. In 1484 a man called Tyrell was accused of murdering **Edward V**.

2 An assassin tried to shoot **George III** while he was at the theatre. The man fired two shots. Both missed by inches and the bullets ended in the wood panel behind the king. What did George do after this near miss?

**a** Stay at the theatre and drop off to sleep.

**b** Faint and have to be carried home.
**c** Order the arrest and execution of the gunman.

**3 Cardinal Reginald Pole** opposed the divorce of **Henry VIII**. The king was furious, but Pole wasn't in the country so Henry couldn't get at him. Never mind … Henry had Pole's mother, the Countess of Salisbury, beheaded instead.

YOU WANT THE HEAD ON A POLE?

NO YOU FOOL, I WANT THE HEAD OFF A POLE!

**4 Elizabeth** I had one serious rival for the throne. Her cousin, **Mary Queen of Scots**. Mary came to England – and Elizabeth had her arrested. She wanted Mary dead but was afraid that people might turn against her if she killed Mary. So she was very sneaky. Elizabeth…

And that was just one of Elizabeth I's *nicer* acts...

# Elizabeth I (1558–1603) – Frizzy Lizzie

## Claim to fame

- Beat the Spanish Armada (with a little help from Francis Drake and the English navy).
- Tried hard to stay young with harsh chemical make-up and hair-dye … but she just ended up bald and toothless.
- Never married … though she had a few flings.

## Mean queen

Elizabeth never married, but she had a few close shaves. (No, not on her head, you fool.) There were some men she came close to marrying several times. The first victim was Lord Dudley…

127

## Like father like daughter

Elizabeth seems to have inherited her father, **Henry VIII's** nasty temper and cruel nature. Did you know…?

- When her sister Mary died, Liz said, 'This is the Lord's doing and it is marvellous in our eyes!' Just like Henry dancing at the news of Catherine's death.
- Ordered the death of **Mary Queen of Scots** … just as Henry had ordered the death of Elizabeth's mother (Anne Boleyn). But at least Elizabeth said 'Sorry' to Mary Queen of Scots' son, **James I**.
- Had no hesitation in executing her best friend, the Earl of Essex … just as Henry had ordered the execution of Thomas More.
- Had a temper like a spoilt child. She punched and kicked William Davison (her secretary) if she couldn't get her own way, and told him to get out of her sight. Just as bad-tempered Henry had cruelly abandoned his loyal servant, Thomas Wolsey, because Wolsey couldn't get him the divorce he wanted.

### Funny fact

Elizabeth I had a tax put on men's beards.

### Fantastic fact

Some people believed that **Elizabeth I** wrote the plays of William Shakespeare. That is nonsense. But it is true that Lizzie watched his plays. The actors had to be very careful what they showed her.

Elizabeth was terrified of being pushed off the throne, so she hated to see scenes where a monarch was overthrown. There's a scene in a Shakespeare play where **Richard II** is deposed. That scene was never performed during Lizzie's reign!

*Did you know…?*
**Elizabeth I** had 80 wigs to cover her baldness. She wasn't the only monarch with hair problems…

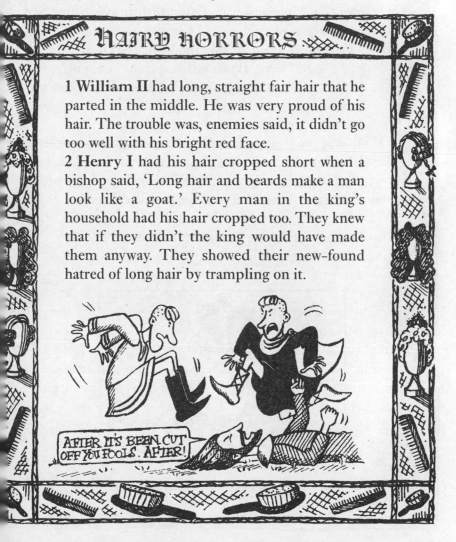

# HAIRY HORRORS

1 **William II** had long, straight fair hair that he parted in the middle. He was very proud of his hair. The trouble was, enemies said, it didn't go too well with his bright red face.

2 **Henry I** had his hair cropped short when a bishop said, 'Long hair and beards make a man look like a goat.' Every man in the king's household had his hair cropped too. They knew that if they didn't the king would have made them anyway. They showed their new-found hatred of long hair by trampling on it.

**3 Edward I's** son, Prince Edward, promised his friend some land. The king was furious. He sent for the prince and gripped a tuft of his hair in each hand. He ripped the hair out by the roots while he told young Ed just what he thought of him. The king kept ripping out the prince's hair until he was too exhausted to carry on.

**4 George II's** son-in-law, the Prince of Orange, had a wig of long, flowing hair. It hid the hump on his back. George said he looked like a baboon.

**5** When **Edward VII** came to the throne in 1901 he was the first monarch to have a beard since **Charles I** (who had his trimmed by the headsman's axe in 1649). No king had risked wearing a beard since. (And no queen either.)

Of course, Charles I's father, had a beard to hide his slobbering mouth…

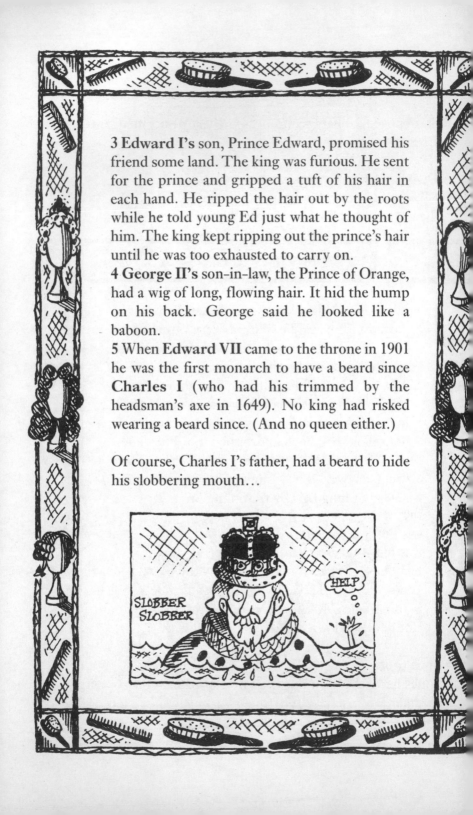

SLOBBER SLOBBER

HELP

# James I (1603–1625) – The Snotty Scot

## Claim to fame

- Son of **Mary Queen of Scots**, who had James's dad murdered then married the murderer. Mary ran off and left James when he was just a few months old. He took the Scottish throne when he was just a year old, and was known as **James VI of Scotland**. A popular choice – he was too young to murder anybody.
- Famous for *not* getting blown up by the Gunpowder Plot.
- When **Liz I** died he took the English throne as well as the Scottish one – the first monarch to rule both countries. But he was known as **James I** of England.

## Foul fact

James had a drunken nurse, so he copied her and grew up a drunkard himself. Unfortunately, he couldn't hold his drink – literally. When he fell ill, his doctors ordered him to drink huge quantities of beer to cool him down. In fact this is what killed him!

## Cruel king

One afternoon, **James VI of Scotland** went out hunting near Perth. He happened to meet a young friend, 15-year-old Alexander. 'Will you come to supper at our castle?' young Alex said.

'I'd love to!' James said.

Alex lived at Gowrie Castle, his older brother's home. James accepted the boy's invitation. (Any chance of a free meal was gratefully accepted by the greedy king.)

Then, after supper, James and Alex started larking about. (Remember there was no television to keep them entertained). The king's soldiers heard the noise and were worried. They rushed into the room to find the two young men wrestling on the floor. The king was panting with excitement, too breathless to stop his soldiers from killing Alex on the spot.

'What did you do that for?' James finally managed to splutter.

'He was trying to kill you, wasn't he?' the Captain of the Guard asked.

James was too embarrassed to deny it. 'Er … aye … well done, Captain. Aye … an evil plot to murder me!'

'A plot? Who was he plotting with?'

'Ah … er … ah … I don't know,' James squirmed.

'Must be his brother,' the Captain nodded.

'Must be,' the king agreed, weakly.

Alexander's older brother, the Earl of Gowrie, was grabbed and quickly put to death. (Gowrie Castle must have looked like Gory Castle by now.)

Then James began to get a bit worried. 'It doesn't do to kill a man without a fair trial' he whinged. 'It doesn't seem fair.' (What he really meant was, 'People will say I'm a murderer.')

'Then we'll give them a trial,' the Captain promised.

And so the dead brothers were taken to Edinburgh. Ten weeks later the corpses were put on trial. They were found guilty. (They didn't have a lot to say in their own defence, of course).

'I sentence you to be hanged by the neck until you are dead,' the judge declared.

The brothers were taken away ... and hanged. (But as they were already dead they probably didn't mind this too much. Not as much as you or I would.)

No one in Scotland really believed James's story, you understand. But no one wanted to argue with the king.

Three years later, **Elizabeth I** died in England. James went south to become king of England.

The people of Scotland might not have been too sorry to lose him. Would you?

**Another foul fact**

**James I's** idea of a joke was to put a frog down the Earl of Pembroke's neck. The Earl got his revenge by putting a pig in the king's bedroom!

**James I** wasn't the only king from Scotland to have a mean historical past...

# James, James, James, James ... AND James!

**1 James I of England and VI of Scotland** wore a thickly padded jacket because he was scared of being stabbed. Not surprising when you remember what happened to his great grandfather, **James III of Scotland**.

**2 James III** fought in the Battle of Sauchieburn and lost. In the battle he was wounded, but he'd probably have lived. Then a priest arrived to help the king. He 'helped' James into the afterlife by stabbing him to death. The priest turned out to be a soldier in disguise.

**3** His son, **James IV of Scotland**, was the last king in Britain to die in battle. Don't feel too sorry for him. It was James IV who had fought against **James III** at the Battle of Sauchieburn, that led to the death of James III. And James III was his dad!

**4 James I of Scotland** was just a twelve-year-old prince when he was captured by pirates in 1406. The pirates sold the prince to the English enemy, **Henry IV**, who kept James prisoner for 16 years before he was ransomed. James's father died of a broken heart – and James became king while still Henry's prisoner. (At least he *survived* those 16 years in English prisons. When he finally got back to Scotland he lived just 15 years before he was assassinated – by a Scot.)

5 Miserable **James II of Scotland** banned football and golf in 1457. 'If the men want to practise a sport then they should try something useful, like archery,' he said. He was killed by an exploding cannon.

# Charles I (1625–1649) – Chopped Charlie

### Claim to fame
- Tried to tell everyone he could do what he wanted because God gave kings their power – this is called

'The Divine Right'. (God must have been looking the other way when Charlie's enemies chopped his head off.)

- Shy and nervous but tried hard to cover this up by acting tough.
- Had a Scottish accent and a squeaky little voice with a slight stammer. His eyes never rested on the people he was talking to but seemed to look through them.

## Charles's famous last words

Charles decided to wear two shirts for his execution. It was a cold day – there was ice on the river. The King didn't want to shiver and look chicken.

He also wanted to make sure he didn't forget the lines for his famous last words. As he stepped on to the scaffold and took a crumpled piece of paper from his pocket, he spoke in a whisper...

*All the world knows I never did begin a war with Parliament. I die a Christian of the Church of England. I will say no more.*

He stretched out an arm, the axe fell and severed the head cleanly. The crowd surged forward and some dipped handkerchiefs in the blood. A newspaper report of the 1649 execution said...

30 January 1649

Today it did not rain. But it was a wet day in London because of all the tears that fell from many eyes

*Did you know…?*

- After his execution, Charles's head was sewn back on to his body so relatives could pay their last respects before it was buried. But he wasn't allowed to rest in peace. The neck-bone of **Charles I** which suffered the chop was later taken from the tomb by Sir Henry Halford. He shocked friends at the dinner-table by using it as a salt cellar!

- Charles's wife, Henrietta, died in France and was buried there. Like Charles, her body wasn't left to rest in peace. It was dug up a hundred years later during the French Revolution.

- Charles's coffin was carried to the funeral covered in a black velvet cloth. On the way, it began to snow and the black cover turned white. 'White for innocence,' many superstitious people muttered.

- Charles I's ghost can be seen in York. He haunts a stone stairway in King's Manor. His ghost is also seen in a bedroom of Vernon House in Farnham, Surrey. That's a couple of hundred miles south of York, so he must be a restless ghost.

- Charles married the 15-year-old Henrietta Maria in 1625 … but he didn't turn up for the wedding ceremony! He stayed in England while his friend, the Duke of Buckingham, acted as a stand-in at the wedding in Notre Dame, Paris.

- When the Scots sold him back to the English to be executed, Charles wasn't treated too badly in Carisbrooke Castle. He had 12 servants, a food waiter, a wine waiter and three cooks. The local people often came to watch him eat!

137

**Test your teacher**

Charles was put on trial for 'treason' after he raised an army and marched against the army of Parliament. Charles had 135 judges. In the end he was found guilty and executed, of course. But how many voted for his death?

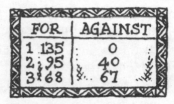

| FOR | | AGAINST |
|---|---|---|
| 1 | 135 | 0 |
| 2 | 95 | 40 |
| 3 | 68 | 67 |

*Answer:* 3 Charles was found guilty by just one vote.

# Charles II (1660–1685) – Cheerful Charlie

## Claim to fame

- Fought for his father in the English Civil War – once escaping after hiding up a tree for days.

- Also fought the Fire of London in 1666 and survived the Great Plague of 1665.
- Became the first king to return after Oliver Cromwell's Commonwealth (Cromwell won the Civil War) had abolished kings and executed **Charles I**. Cromwell's Britain was so boring the people were glad to have a king back. And Charlie Two brought them the brightness they wanted. They called him 'The Merry Monarch'.

**Funny fact**
**Charles II** was keen on astronomy and had a telescope set up at the Tower of London. One day his view was suddenly blocked. A passing raven had splattered the telescope. Charles was mad. 'The ravens have to go!' he said.

His Astronomer Royal, Sir John Flamstead, said, 'But it is terribly unlucky to kill a Tower raven. If the ravens go, the Tower will fall and you will lose your kingdom ... you've only just got it back.'

Charles thought about this. 'The ravens can stay in the Tower – the Royal Observatory can go to Greenwich.' The Observatory has been there ever since – and the ravens are still at the Tower.

*Did you know…?*
When a Tower of London raven dies it is buried in the moat. One raven lived so long it was given a pet name, James Crow. It survived 44 years – which is exactly twice as long as **Edward V** and his brother **Richard** (the murdered 'Princes in the Tower') added together. It's clearly more healthy outside than inside the Tower of London!

## Clumsy clots

**Charles II** collapsed while he was being shaved. Unfortunately there was a doctor near and he gave the usual treatment – he 'bled' the king of an armful of blood. (Letting blood out of the body was supposed to let out the badness – this was called 'bleeding' a patient.) Charles began to get better *despite* this treatment but collapsed again four days later. His doctor bled him again and again – the king got worse and worse.

In fact, Charles had a kidney disease. He needed as much blood as possible to cope with it. The *very last thing* a doctor should do is *bleed* a patient with that illness. Charles's doctor almost certainly shortened the king's life by a long way.

## Foul fact

**Charles II** gathered the dust from Egyptian mummies and rubbed it into his body. He believed that some of their greatness would rub off on to him. In turn his own greatness was supposed to help others…

# Kingly cures

For hundreds of years, people believed that the touch of a monarch would cure a common disease called *scrofula*. **Charles II** touched 92,000 people in his lifetime. He didn't manage to cure any of them – but the idea did manage to *kill* several of them.

In 1684, there was such a crowd waiting for a ticket to get the royal touch that in the sudden rush for tickets six people were killed.

**Elizabeth I** was particularly brave about 'touching'. A writer of the time described how … 'she first prayed, then pressed the sores and ulcers of the sick, boldly and without disgust.'

# James II (1685–1688)– Dim Jim

### Claim to fame
- Tried to turn Britain back into a Catholic country.
- Thrown out of Britain after three years on the throne. He tried to escape but was recognized by some fishermen. His second escape attempt succeeded.
- Went to France and never returned.

### Cruel king
**James II** had the Duke of Monmouth's head chopped off for leading a rebellion. Monmouth gave the executioner six guineas so the man wouldn't make a mess of it (as he had with Lord Russell). The executioner chopped – and missed. After a few goes he eventually got the head off...

And so that's what happened. Monmouth's dead head was stuck back on to his body, sewn in place, and his portrait painted.

The picture was finished and Monmouth was buried.

The finished portrait can be seen in London's National Portrait Gallery.

**Foul fact**
**James II** was thrown out of England and had to spend the rest of his life in France. He was buried there in the Church of the English Benedictines, but couldn't rest in peace. First the coffin was moved to a church of St Germain, then, a hundred years later, it was dug up and destroyed during the French Revolution.

## CURIOUS CLOTHES

**1 Henry VIII** wasn't quite as fat as he appears in his pictures. He wore padded clothes because they were warmer in the draughty castles of that time.

**2 Caroline**, wife of **George IV**, couldn't dress herself properly. A lady-in-waiting claimed she put her stockings on inside out and back-to-front ... and she didn't change them very often.

**3 William IV** wore thick rubber overshoes – galoshes – because he thought it would stop him getting a chill.

**4 Elizabeth I** had very few clothes when she was a child. She made up for this when she became queen. Liz owned a thousand dresses, many of them covered with a fortune in jewels – so thick with jewels, in fact, that they stood up by themselves. Liz had all this fortune stuck in her wardrobes but sent her

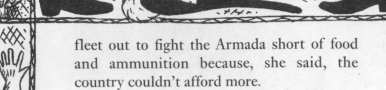

fleet out to fight the Armada short of food and ammunition because, she said, the country couldn't afford more.

**5 James I** followed Elizabeth and had his own curious obsession – but not with dresses. He bought countless pairs of gloves. Sir Anthony Weldon described how…

WIPE WIPE

HE NEVER WASHED HIS HANDS, ONLY RUBBED HIS FINGER ENDS SLIGHTLY WITH THE WET END OF A NAPKIN

James probably had a skin disease which is why he always wore gloves, and found it too painful to wash his hands.

**Queen Mary II** accidentally started a fashion among lawyers which has lasted to this day…

# William III and Mary II (1689–1702) – Little and Large

### Claim to fame

- **William of Orange** (a place in France, not the fruit) was married to the Protestant daughter of **James II, Mary II**. Parliament asked her to take over her dad's throne as queen. William said, 'If you don't make me king then we'll go straight back to Holland.'

- Mary was four-and-a-half inches taller than William.

- The couple shared the throne for four years. Then Mary died and Will ruled alone for another eight.

**Funny fact**

William was small. Mary was large. She didn't take his arm when they walked together. Instead he took her arm. Someone said, 'He hung on her arm like a bracelet.'

**Fantastic fact**

When Mary died, all the lawyers wore black robes as a sign of mourning. And they haven't stopped wearing black in court ever since.

**Foul fact**

William was out riding one day in 1702 when his horse, Sorrel, stumbled on a molehill. The king fell off and broke his collar bone. The injury became infected and William died.

The supporters of **King James II** were delighted. They thought the mole that dug the hole that killed the king was a wonderful creature. Ever since, the supporters of the Stuart family have drunk the health of 'the little gentleman in black velvet'.

CHEERS TO THE LITTLE GENTLEMAN IN BLACK VELVET

But **William III** wasn't the only monarch to have trouble with a four-legged friend...

148

# Rotten riders

The Roman emperor Caligula was famous for making Incitatus a senator – that's a bit like a Prime Minister. And Incitatus was his favourite horse! But English kings and queens had strange experiences with horses too…

1 King **Alexander III of Scotland** learned the hard way that horses can't fly. He died when his horse jumped over a cliff as they were out riding at night.

2 **William the Conqueror's** horse reared up when it saw a hot cinder. William struck his stomach on the front of the saddle – the 'pommel'. His internal injuries were so serious he died soon after.

3 The daughter of **Elizabeth II, Princess Anne** rode for the 1976 British Olympic Eventing team in Montreal. She didn't fall off (well, not *that* time) but she did fall *in*. She fell *in* love with fellow-rider Captain Mark Phillips and married him. And Captain Phillips has an ancestor called, believe it or not, Miss Horsey de Horsey.

4 Emily Davison wanted women to be able to vote for Members of Parliament. She was a member of a 'Votes for Women' group

called 'suffragettes.' They needed publicity. So Ms Davison decided to stop King **George V**'s racehorse in the great race, the Derby. As the horses galloped into the straight at nearly 40 miles an hour, she jumped out in front of George's horse.

The horse didn't stop. Ms Davison didn't live to enjoy the publicity she got – or the huge funeral parade with 2,000 suffragettes escorting the coffin.

**5** Shakespeare's play about **Richard III** shows the king fighting to the death on foot, crying, 'My Kingdom for a horse!' Richard III's coffin was said to have been used as a horse trough for many years after his death. Maybe he should have cried, 'My coffin for a horse!'

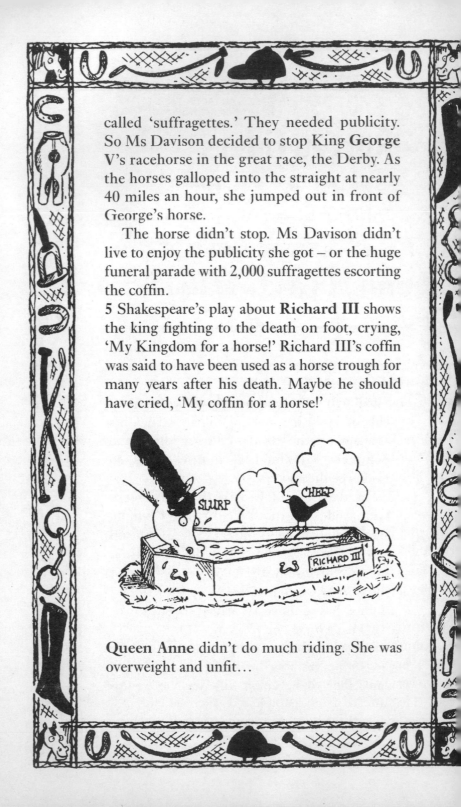

**Queen Anne** didn't do much riding. She was overweight and unfit…

# Anne I (1702–1714) – Br-ann-dy

### Claim to fame
- The first monarch to see a single Parliament for both England and Scotland.
- Her general, the **Duke of Marlborough**, won some glorious victories for her. She sacked him.
- She was fond of food and addicted to brandy.

### Foul fact
Anne had 17 children. They all died as babies except one, William. When William reached the age of 11 he must have realized he was a bit odd, living so long. So he popped his clogs, poor kid.

### Funny fact
Anne's husband, George, was boring.

Very boring.

Very, very boring.

He suffered from asthma and when he had an attack he breathed very heavily. Someone unkindly suggested that he did this to prove to everyone he was still alive. If he didn't pant loudly he might be carried off and buried by mistake.

Over a hundred years later, **Queen Victoria** remembered **Prince George** as, 'the very stupid and unimportant husband of Queen Anne.'

**Frivolous fact**
**Anne I's** husband, George, didn't have much work to do ruling the country, so he spent his time making model ships. When Anne came to the throne she made him Lord High Admiral.

Anne herself preferred dominoes, which is possibly why she sat and grew fat...

**Fat fact**
**Anne** was so fond of food she developed gout – swollen feet caused by eating too much rich food. She was the only monarch who had to be carried to her coronation. And when she was buried, her huge coffin was practically square.

And she wasn't the only monarch with a thing about food...

# Greedy guts

**1 Henry VIII** was famous for his feasts. In the end he grew so fat that ropes and pulleys had to be used to haul him upstairs and into bed.

**2 George I** died after gorging himself on fruit one night. (Perhaps it was melons, though some say strawberries and oranges). The next morning he had a cup of hot chocolate for breakfast and that finished him off.

**3** Amazingly, his son, **George II** died after a breakfast of … guess what? Yes, *hot chocolate*. The message is, 'If you're a king called George then stay off the hot chocolate!' But **George VI** had a cup of *hot chocolate* for his supper. Next morning his servant found him dead. It seems some kings never learn.

**4 John I** was upset after he lost all of his crown jewels in a travelling accident. He decided to cheer himself up by stuffing himself with peaches and fresh cider. After two days he wasn't upset any more. He was dead. The over-eating killed him.

**5 James I** was probably the messiest monarch. A visitor said, *His tongue was too large for his mouth which made him drink very badly as if eating his drink which came out into the cup from each side of his mouth.*

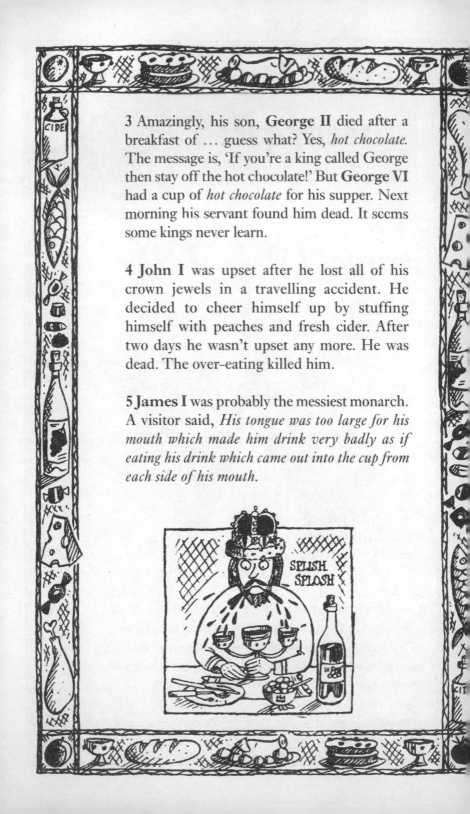

# George I (1714–1727) – German George

## Claim to fame
- Spoke only German (or French) and never bothered to learn English.
- Parliament loved this because it meant *they* could rule the country – something they'd been wanting for hundreds of years. And at least, they said, he was better than the Stuarts.
- Also famous for his cruel treatment of his wife.

## Cruel king
**Prince George** married **Dorothea**. He had lots of girlfriends and he thought that was all right. Then he heard that Dorothea had a boyfriend. That was most definitely *not* all right! (This is not fair, you understand, but other kings – such as **Henry VIII** – thought the same way.)

The man she had been flirting with was the handsome Count Konigsmark. Dorothea's friends knew what was going on and went running to George with the story. Fine friends they turned out to be! Prince George ordered the count to leave the country the next day and never return.

155

'See him one more time,' the treacherous friends urged Dorothea. 'Give him just one goodbye kiss.'

Dorothea said, 'Yes. Bring him to my room.'

The fiendish friends smirked and set about their work. Count Konigsmark came to say farewell. He kissed the lonely Dorothea's hand, then marched off into exile.

He was never seen again … well, that's not strictly true.

George had Dorothea kept a prisoner in that palace. Later, much later, after George and Dorothea died, the palace was rebuilt. Count Konigsmark was seen again after all those years. Where?

1 In Dorothea's dressing room.

2 Working as a servant in the kitchen.

3 He turned up as a guest at the funeral.

*Answer:* 1 His corpse was underneath the floorboards of Dorothea's dressing room. He must have been strangled the moment he left Dorothea's bedroom and his body hidden underneath the floorboards. Dorothea spent 32 years a prisoner in that palace. She must have often wondered what had happened to the handsome count, little dreaming he was closer than she ever thought.

**Fantastic fact**

**George II** hated his father **George I** for imprisoning Dorothea. Not only was she kept in Ahlden Castle but she was banned from seeing her children (including **Prince George**) ever again. It is said that the Prince tried to swim the Ahlden Castle moat in order to see his mum. He failed. During George I's lifetime no one was ever told what had happened to his queen.

## Foul fact

When Dorothea died, George left her unburied for six months! And when he finally set off to arrange her funeral … he died on the way!

**George I** wasn't the only Royal to want his spouse dead…

# Manic marriages

**1 Mary I** was married to **Spanish King Philip**. It was a marriage that was mainly arranged to bring peace between the two kingdoms, but Mary actually loved Philip. Unfortunately Phil didn't love Mary and left her. He complained of the sickening smell that came from her nostrils. (This was probably a disease that she inherited from her father **Henry VIII** as a result of his bad lifestyle.)

**2 John** I divorced his wife, Isabella of Gloucester, and married Isabella of Angouleme. (This saved him having to learn a new name.) Isabella Two was just twelve years old.

WILL YOU MARRY ME?

ONLY IF YOU MARRY DOLLY AS WELL

**3 Edward II's** wife led a rebellion – against Edward! Can you blame her? One of the first things Edward did when he married Isabella was to give their best wedding presents away to his best friend, Piers Gaveston. Isabella's lover, Roger Mortimer, probably had Edward murdered. It was said he carried a knife to kill her with, if it became necessary. If he had no weapon he'd 'crush her with his teeth.'

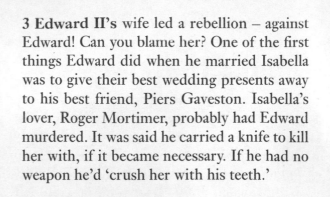

AND IF MY TEETH HAVE FALLEN OUT THEN I'LL GUM HER TO DEATH!

**4 Henry VIII** had six wives but chose to be buried next to the third – Jane Seymour. Romantics say, 'This was the one he loved most of all.' But was it?

His last wife was still alive when he died, so he couldn't be buried next to her.

Divorced wife, Anne of Cleves, was still alive – so he couldn't be buried next to her either.

Anne Boleyn and Catherine Howard had been beheaded – so he wouldn't want to be buried next to any of those four bits.

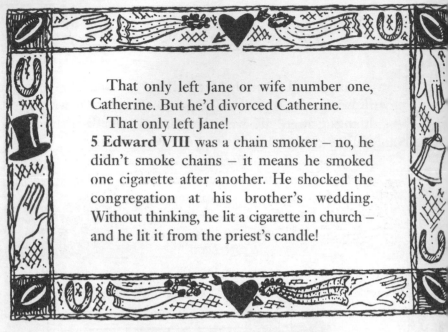

That only left Jane or wife number one, Catherine. But he'd divorced Catherine.

That only left Jane!

**5 Edward VIII** was a chain smoker – no, he didn't smoke chains – it means he smoked one cigarette after another. He shocked the congregation at his brother's wedding. Without thinking, he lit a cigarette in church – and he lit it from the priest's candle!

# George II (1727–1760) – Greedy George

## Claim to fame

- Added Canada and India to the British Empire.
- Never very popular with the British people because he seemed to like Germany more than Britain.
- A bad-tempered man who kicked his coat and wig about when in a rage.

**Funny fact**

**Queen Caroline,** George's wife, was even unpopular with the kids in the street. They made up a silly street rhyme about her that went...

*Queen, Queen Caroline,*
*Dipped her nose in turpentine,*
*Turpentine to make it shine,*
*Poor Queen Caroline.*

**Foul fact**

George II ordered the very last beheading in the Tower of London. Lord Lovat was 80 years old and had supported a Stuart rebellion, so he had to go. Lovat was determined to enjoy his execution. He shouted insults to the crowd on his way to the scaffold. A stand was built for spectators. It collapsed under the weight of numbers. The gruesome spectators went to watch an old man die – they didn't expect to die themselves ... but 20 of them did when they were crushed in the accident.

**Fantastic fact**

You could buy a ticket to watch **George II** and the royal family eat their Sunday dinner.

**Quick quiz**

The Prime Minister told **Prince George** that his father, **George I,** had died and the Prince was now **King George II.** What did the new king say?

1 At last!
2 How tragic!
3 You liar!

*Answer:* **3** Prime Minister Walpole broke the news. George II hated Walpole and thought this was a cruel Walpole joke. It wasn't.

*Did you know…?*

**George II** was the last British monarch to lead his army into battle. Sounds heroic? Unfortunately it wasn't. If there had been a newspaper reporter on the spot then his article might have looked something like this…

## GERMAN GEORGE - A JOKE ON A GEE-GEE

Yesterday the English Army beat the gallant French at Dettingen in Germany - but not before the Brits' German king made a complete ass of himself!

The desperate Brit army faced up to the gallant French who only outnumbered the enemy two to one. Suddenly a fat figure in a white wig appeared on a horse. "C'est Georgie!" the fantastic French cried. Sure enough the Brit King George (60) had turned up to personally lead his troops into battle.

That's when Georgie's gee-gee decided it didn't fancy the look of the fierce French fighters. It turned round and began trotting back the way it had come.

French and Brit troops watched in amazement as the king tried to reel in the reins with all his might . . . and mane. But the more he tried to stop it the faster the horse ran away. It was last seen bolting back to Britain as fast as its cowardly legs could carry it.

A French soldier joked, "Even our old King Louis XIV could ride better than that - and he died back in 1715!"

"That's right," his pal joined in. "George had a very long rein - that's something the French don't allow their kings!"

More than half an hour passed before George made his way back to the front of his troops.

He was on foot!

A Brit Brigadier had to admit, "He looked a saddle 'n lonely figure."

Britain may have won the battle, but the French laughed themselves hoarse . . . or should that be **horse**?

Are the French down-hearted? Neigh!

**Funny fact**

**Queen Caroline** was determined to look impressive at her coronation. She not only wore all of her many jewels, she also borrowed or hired all the diamonds and pearls she could get her hands on. She must have looked like a Christmas tree. In fact, her dress was so stiff with jewels that she couldn't lift it to kneel down. It had to be fitted with strings so it could be lifted up, like a Venetian blind.

But at least the coronation wasn't the sort of disaster that doomed some monarchs...

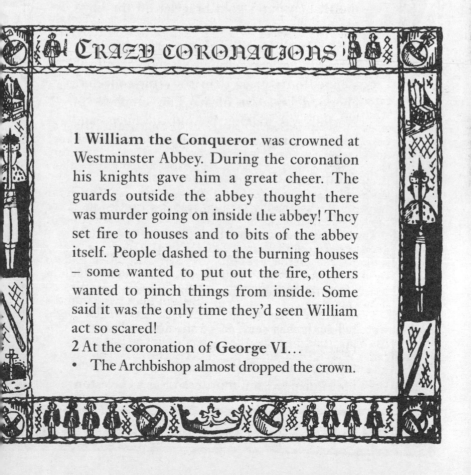

# CRAZY CORONATIONS

**1 William the Conqueror** was crowned at Westminster Abbey. During the coronation his knights gave him a great cheer. The guards outside the abbey thought there was murder going on inside the abbey! They set fire to houses and to bits of the abbey itself. People dashed to the burning houses – some wanted to put out the fire, others wanted to pinch things from inside. Some said it was the only time they'd seen William act so scared!

**2** At the coronation of **George VI**...

- The Archbishop almost dropped the crown.

- The king couldn't read the oath because a bishop put his thumb over the words.
- The Lord Chamberlain nearly smacked the king on the chin with the sword of state.
- And, when George tried to stand up, he was jerked back because a bishop was standing on his robe.

3 Because **John** had lost the crown jewels, there was no crown to put on the head of the next king, **Henry III**. But Henry was just nine years old (and only had a little head) so the Bishop put a gold bracelet on the boy's head instead.

4 **Elizabeth I** walked down a rich new blue carpet to her coronation. No sooner had she stepped on a piece than souvenir-collectors chopped bits out of it. The Duchess of Norfolk was walking behind the queen and kept tripping as she caught her foot in the holes.

5 **Edward II** left the arrangements for his coronation to his friend, Piers Gaveston. Piers spent a lot of time getting himself dressed for the event – some said he looked more splendid than the king – and not enough time sorting out the important things. So, when the nobles came to the coronation feast, it wasn't ready. The starving nobles had to wait until night before it was served – and, after all that, it tasted awful. Four years later one of the nobles, the Earl of Warwick, got his own back. He kidnapped and murdered Piers Gaveston.

6 'Edward III had himself crowned 'King of France' and he started a fashion. All English monarchs had themselves crowned 'Ruler of France' ... even though they weren't. The Dukes of Normandy and Aquitane would have had to come to the coronations of English monarchs and accept the English as their rulers. Of course they never did. So each English coronation had actors playing the parts of these two dukes. The last time it happened was at **George III's** coronation in 1761. The scene was quite ridiculous. As the king had the crown placed on his head, the real lords placed coronets on their own heads ... while the actors slapped on their caps! And that wasn't the only crazy thing that happened in the reign of George III...

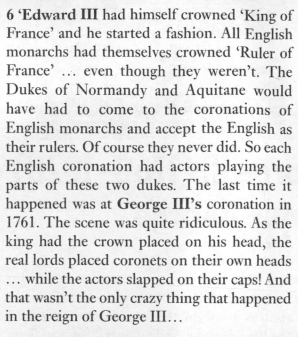

# George III (1760–1820) – Simple George

## Claim to fame

- First king of Britain and Ireland ... but his armed forces managed to lose him the American colonies. They did beat the French Navy (at Trafalgar) and Napoleon's army (at Waterloo) to win the Napoleonic Wars, so that made up for it.
- Famous for his periods of insanity when his son took over as 'Prince Regent'.
- Liked a 'simple' life compared to many previous kings. Loved music – hated Shakespeare. Bought simple little Buckingham Palace to live in.

## Foul fact

George III is known for his madness, though his mental illness only affected him for short periods of the 60 years he was on the throne. But during those periods he couldn't rule a line never mind a country. At different times during his illness he...

- Ended every sentence he spoke with the word 'peacock'. (He tried to open parliament with a speech which began,

'My Lords and peacocks…')

- Believed that London was flooded and ordered a yacht.
- Wore a pillowcase round his head.
- 'Adopted' the new-born Prince Octavius, who was, in fact, a pillow.

- Told the queen that *she* had been mad for 30 years.
- Believed that he himself was dead and wore black as a sign of mourning for 'that good man, George III'.

Stories grew about George's insanity. One said that he was riding in his carriage one day when he ordered the coachman, 'Stop! I see Emperor Frederick the Great over there!' The coach stopped and George stepped down. He walked over to a chestnut tree and shook 'hands' with one of the branches before chatting to the emperor for a while. But this famous story is probably *untrue*.

There was one person who spread the worst lies and rumours about George III's madness. His own son, **Prince George**. The Prince would go around London clubs giving details of his father's illness and even doing a cruel imitation of his sick father.

# George's tale of terror

The butler lifted George's cases down from the carriage and passed them to a footman. 'Take them to the Brown Room,' he ordered.

The footman's eyes widened. 'The Brown Room! Surely…'

The butler's face hardened. 'Don't argue, man. His Highness will be sleeping in the Brown Room tonight! Now get a move on!'

King George shook his head. White powder from his wig drifted down in the calm evening air. 'What was he so frightened about?' the king asked the butler.

The thin man in the black suit rubbed his hands and attempted a thin smile. 'A silly legend – a superstition.'

'About the Brown Room?' the king demanded. 'What about it?'

The butler sighed and spread his hands wide. 'Just some local legend about Dorothy Walpole who used to live here at Raynham Hall…'

'Robert Walpole's daughter? The Old Prime Minister?' the king asked as he began to walk towards the gloomy doorway of the old house.

'His sister, your Highness,' the butler said. 'A sad case. She went mad when her husband left her and they took her children away from her. She spent most of her time in the Brown Room. Died of smallpox in 1721.'

'I see,' the king nodded and marched up the dark oak stairs. 'Sixty-five years ago. The room should be safe from infection by now, eh?'

The butler rubbed his hands and smiled that tight smile again.

'Absolutely, your Highness.'

168

The king nodded and walked into the Brown Room. The footman stood unpacking the king's case. 'So,' George said quietly. 'Dorothy Walpole died of smallpox in this room, eh?'

'Some people say that, your Highness,' the man muttered.

The king walked towards him. 'Some people say that? What do other people say?'

The footman carried on unpacking and licked his lips nervously. 'Some say she was standing at the top of the stairs and she fell ... some say she was pushed.'

'Murder, eh?' the king said. 'No doubt she comes back to haunt the house and seek revenge?'

'No doubt, your Highness,' the man replied.

'Hah!' George exploded. 'Then it's just as well I do not believe in ghosts.'

'As you say, your Highness,' the footman said and, bowing low, he backed towards the door of the room.

George stretched and looked at the comfortable bed. After a tiring journey through the Norfolk countryside he felt he deserved an early night. He knew he'd sleep well.

It was wonderfully quiet in the country after the bustle of London. He slipped between the covers of the bed and was asleep within moments.

He never knew what woke him in the middle of the night. Perhaps it was a small sound, perhaps it was the sudden breath of chill air. But he sat up, suddenly awake.

Someone was moving in his room. 'Who's there?' he whispered.

The figure turned. It was a woman. Her hair was wild and her face deathly pale. As she moved towards him he could see that her dress was brown.

'What do you want?' the king demanded. He tried to sound bold but his voice trembled.

As she came closer, he scrambled to get out of the bed but the bedclothes became tangled round his legs. As she reached him it seemed she must step on his huddled figure. He closed his eyes, felt a bitter chill pass through his body. Then ... nothing. He opened his eyes. He was alone in the room.

He didn't wait to look for his dressing-gown. He tumbled out of the door into the candle-lit corridor and staggered to the room of his host, Lord Townshend.

The startled lord looked at the man in nightgown and nightcap. For a while he thought his king was suffering from one of his fits of madness. But the king seemed sane enough as he said, 'Sir ... I do not like the company in this house. If you will excuse me I will leave.'

'Now, your Highness?'

'Now! I will not spend another moment in this house! Have my bags packed. I shall be waiting in the carriage.'

And, with that, the terrified king fled down the old oak staircase and back to the safety of his London home.

'I will never return... ever,' he swore. And he never did.

But Dorothy's ghost did, and it has been seen many times at Raynham Hall over the last 200 years.

**Funny fact**
'History repeats itself,' they say.
- **George II** married a German, Caroline, who came to England and was very unpopular.
- **George III** married a German, **Charlotte**, who came to England and was very unpopular.

The new **Queen Charlotte** had a nose that tilted upwards. The cruel crowds shouted 'Pug!' at her, meaning 'pug dog'.

# Peculiar partners

**1** Caroline, wife of **George II**, wanted to walk with her husband but had painful legs as a result of rheumatism. To help ease the pain she dipped her legs in freezing mud.

I WISH SHE WOULDN'T DO THAT

**2** When Caroline lay dying, the doctors were operating on her – without an anaesthetic, of course – and she suddenly told them to stop. They stopped. Caroline wasn't in pain, she was bursting with laughter. One of the doctors had leaned too close to a candle and set his wig on fire.

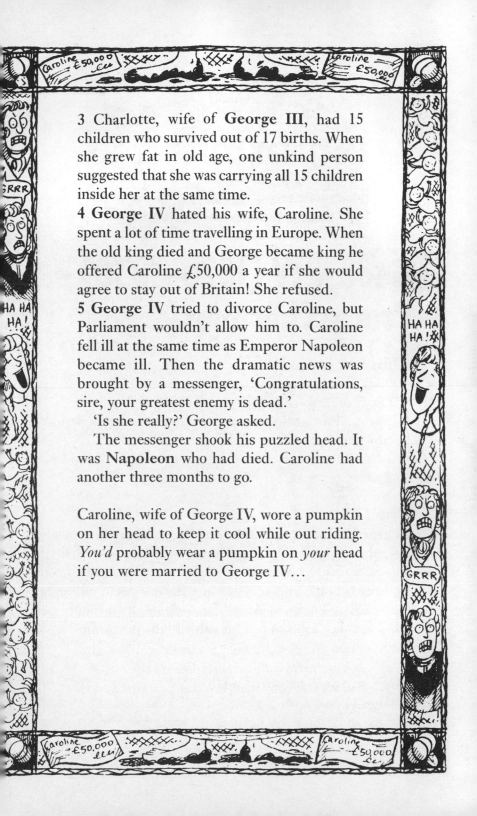

**3** Charlotte, wife of **George III**, had 15 children who survived out of 17 births. When she grew fat in old age, one unkind person suggested that she was carrying all 15 children inside her at the same time.

**4 George IV** hated his wife, Caroline. She spent a lot of time travelling in Europe. When the old king died and George became king he offered Caroline £50,000 a year if she would agree to stay out of Britain! She refused.

**5 George IV** tried to divorce Caroline, but Parliament wouldn't allow him to. Caroline fell ill at the same time as Emperor Napoleon became ill. Then the dramatic news was brought by a messenger, 'Congratulations, sire, your greatest enemy is dead.'

'Is she really?' George asked.

The messenger shook his puzzled head. It was **Napoleon** who had died. Caroline had another three months to go.

Caroline, wife of George IV, wore a pumpkin on her head to keep it cool while out riding. *You'd* probably wear a pumpkin on *your* head if you were married to George IV…

# George IV (1820–1830) – Prince Charmless

### Claim to fame
- Took little interest in government.
- Generally lazy and enjoyed rich living.
- Spent a lot of time standing in for the king (as Regent) while his father, **George III**, was ill.
- Was Prince of Wales for longer than he was king and was always known as 'Prinny'.

### Cruel king
**George IV** was fat. When he was Prince of Wales someone published a poem which called him a 'fat Adonis of fifty'. The poet was locked in prison for two years for this insult. Another poet took his revenge by writing a poem calling fat George 'The Prince of Wales'. The second poet, Lamb, was sensible enough not to put his name to the poem and stayed out of prison.

### Your money or your wife?
**George IV** loved the actress Maria Fitzherbert. She wasn't so sure about him. So he said he would kill himself if she

didn't marry him. He pretended to stab himself – but his doctor probably just made a little nick in his side before Maria arrived. The trick worked – she promised to marry him on the spot.

But Maria was a Catholic. Members of Parliament were horrified when they heard the future queen was a Catholic. They wanted him to marry his German cousin, Caroline. George refused.

Members of Parliament knew that George owed a lot of people a lot of money. They offered to pay all his debts – if he would give up his wife and marry Caroline instead. Your money ... or your wife?

What did Prince George do?

*Answer:* Agreed to marry Caroline and give up Maria.

**Funny fact**
**George IV** used to tell such big lies that he began to believe them himself. He used to say that he had led a marvellous charge at the battle of Waterloo. He hadn't. The Duke of Wellington had been in command at Waterloo. If listeners looked doubtful when George told this story, the king would turn to the Duke and say, 'Isn't that so, Wellington?'

The crafty Duke replied carefully, 'I have often heard you say so, your Majesty.'

**Foul fact**

**George IV**'s over-eating killed him. He died of the strain on his heart from being overweight … not to mention dropsy (a heart and kidney disease) … not forgetting gout … and remember the gallstones … and of course blindness … as well as being doped up with a drug called laudanum (a sleeping drug).

So **George III**'s third son, **William IV,** came sailing to the throne…

# William IV (1830–1837) – Sailor Bill

### Claim to fame
- Spent most of his life in the navy.
- Was 65 when he came to the throne.
- Like his father he fell in love with an actress ... and, like his father, had to give her up. But not until they'd had ten children.

### Funny fact
**William IV** didn't expect to be made king. He thought it was great fun when he came to the throne in 1830 at the age of 65. He had a great time riding out in his carriage so the people could see him. If he saw someone respectable walking along, he would stop and offer them a lift.

### William ... who?
**William IV** is usually one of Britain's forgotten kings. His wife had lived during the years when the French were taking their kings and queens to the guillotine. She was afraid the same would happen to William and her. Her prayers were

filled with hopes that she would be brave when her turn came to be executed. (It never did, of course.) Still, she's remembered in Australia because a famous Australian town is named after her.

## Rame that place!

Can *you* decide where was named after whom?

1 Maryland was named after…    **a** Victoria

2 New York was named after…    **b** The wife of William IV

3 Virginia State (USA) was named after…    **c** James II

4 Adelaide was named after…    **d** Elizabeth I

5 A London station was named after…    **e** The wife of Charles

*Answer:*

1 Maryland was named after … the wife of Charles I (e).

2 New York was named after … James II (when he was Duke of York (c).

3 Virginia State (USA) was named after … Elizabeth I (the Virgin Queen) (d).

4 Adelaide was named after … the wife of William IV (b).

5 A London station was named after … Victoria (a).

### Funny fact

A baby was born in Exeter on the very day that **Edward VIII** came to the throne, so her parents decided to name her 'Coronation'. Twenty years later, Coronation married Mr Street … and became Coronation Street.

# Victoria I (1837–1901) – Misery Vee

### Claim to fame

- Reigned while the British Empire grew. Eventually Victoria was the empress of a quarter of all the people in the world.
- For all the riches this brought, many British people lived terrible lives in slums.
- Married Albert and had nine children – then he died and Vic spent the last 40 years of her life moaning about it.

### Mean queen

**Victoria** had a lady-in-waiting, Lady Flora. Lady Flora's stomach began to swell and gossips said the unmarried lady was expecting a baby. Lady Flora denied it but vicious Victoria believed the rumours and gave the poor woman a hard time. In fact, Lady Flora's swelling was a cancer of the liver. She died two months later. The young queen's cruel treatment of Lady Flora made her very unpopular for the first few years of her reign.

180

**Fantastic fact**

There were seven assassination attempts on **Victoria's** life, mostly with pistols. Fortunately for Vic, they were rotten shots. Incredibly, one man who shot at Victoria as she drove down London's Mall, came back the same time next day. Victoria drove past the same place at the same time and he was able to take a second pot at her.

**Foul fact**

Albert died but **Victoria** still had his clothes laid out for him every morning as if he were alive and going to wake up and get dressed. This went on for 40 years! After that, Vic must have realized Bert wasn't going to be waking up ever again.

**Funny fact**

**Victoria** lived to the age of 81 – most of those years as Queen of Britain – yet she never spoke English perfectly. Like her Hanover family ancestors, her natural language was German. On 23 September 1896, Victoria made a special note in her diary. She had broken a record. She had ruled one day longer than **George III**. So what? So that made her the longest-ruling monarch Britain had ever had at the time. And she still had five years to live.

*Did you know…?*
**Victoria** won prizes at Cruft's dog show … at least, her dogs did.

And she wasn't the only monarch who was daft over dogs…

## CROWNED CANINES

1 **Charles I** took his dog with him to his execution.

I LIKE A NICE MEATY CHOP

WAG WAG

**2 Mary Queen of Scots** was followed to her exccution by her pet dog. After her head was lopped off, the dog ran out from under her petticoats. It then lay down in the space between the dead queen's head and her body.

**3 Elizabeth II** likes corgis ... the corgis are not always so keen on each other. She was once bitten while trying to break up a dog-fight.

**4 Princess Annc,** the daughter of **Elizabeth II,** has a stranger link with monarchic mutts. She lived in a house that was haunted by a headless black dog.

**5 Richard II** had a faithful greyhound that followed him everywhere. A faithful and very *intelligent* greyhound. For, when Richard was captured by Henry, the dog crossed the hall and stood by Henry's side. His new master went on to become **Henry IV.**

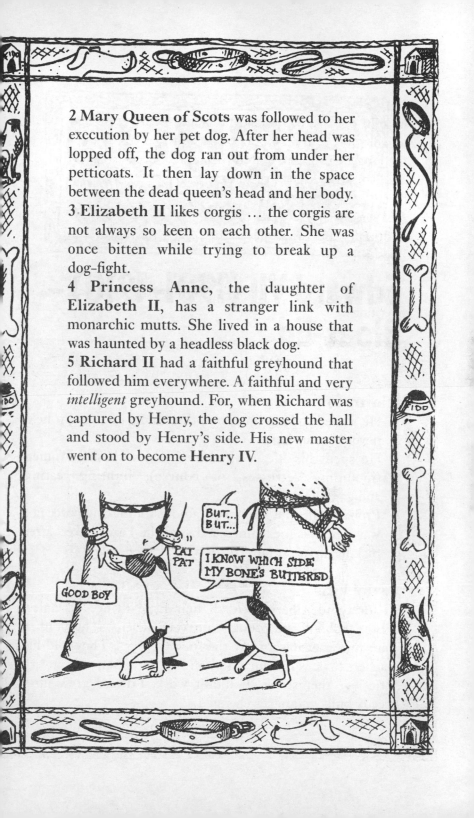

TIGER   FLAMINGO   MANSERVANT   FRIEND

# Edward VII (1901–1910) – Bloat-Ed

## Claim to fame

- He waited so long for his mother to die he thought he'd never become king.
- He spent his life as Prince of Wales chasing women (including actresses, of course), hunting, eating and gambling.
- Probably the first king to be famous for making peace not war – he was nicknamed 'Edward the Peacemaker' after making an important treaty with France.

## Cruel king

Victoria and Albert decided their little Prince of Wales, Edward, should be brought up very strictly. They didn't want him growing up like the four Georges. They told his teachers to be very firm with him and they showed him very little love themselves. It didn't work. Edward grew up a greedy bully and never changed.

As a child he had no friends of his own age. When parents sent their children to play with Prince Edward, he was so rotten to them they never went again.

When he was 17, he tormented his man-servant by pouring wax over his new uniform, pouring water over his clean shirt and punching him on the nose.

Like a lot of bullies he could dish out injury to others, but couldn't take it. Everyone called Edward 'Tum-tum' but no one ever called him that to his face. Until … one night, in a billiards club, he was having a game with Sir Frederick Johnstone.

'You are very drunk,' Edward sneered at Sir Fred.

'And you are very fat, Tum-tum,' his partner replied.

There was a horrified silence in the billiard room. Would Edward laugh?

What did Edward do?
1 Laugh.
2 Say even ruder things to Sir Fred.
3 Have his partner thrown out of the club and banned.

*Answer:* 3 Edward was furious and had the poor Sir Fred thrown out and disgraced.

**Fantastic fact**
Edward began chasing girls at a very early age. In fact he was six years old when he started.

**Foul fact**

On a hunting trip to Egypt, Ed made sure he had enough to eat by shooting plenty of wild birds – including flamingos. And, in case they went thirsty, the hunting party took 7,000 bottles of wine.

**Funny fact**

Edward liked practical jokes. He once left a present in a friend's bed – a dead seagull.

A nastier trick was to ask a friend to look closely into his eyes and see cigar smoke coming from them. The friend leaned forward, hands on the table, while Edward sucked in smoke from the cigar. As the friend stared into the king's eyes, Edward brought the glowing end of the cigar down on to the back of his friend's hand.

Ha! Ha! Laugh?

Er … no, not really.

His son, **George V**, wasn't a bundle of laughs either…

186

# George V (1910–1936) – Windsor the First

## Claim to fame

- Was king when Britain went to war with Germany in 1914. With their German ancestors, the royal family were afraid that the British people would overthrow them. The German leader, Kaiser William II, was George's cousin.
- Changed the family name from the German Wettin, to Windsor – the name the present royal family still has.
- Like his ancestor, **William IV**, he had a career in the Navy because he never expected to become king.

## Cruel king

Victoria had descendants who ruled much of Europe at the beginning of the twentieth century. Many European monarchs were related to **George V**. One group of close relatives was the Russian royal family.

In 1917, the Russian people decided to get rid of George's cousin, Tsar Nicholas. Nicholas sent a message to George.

'Can the Russian royal family come to Britain for safety … please?'

February 1917                                    Petrograd

Dear George

Hope you and the family are keeping well. How's the weather over in Britain? It's snowing here in Russia.

And how's the war going? Should be over by Christmas my generals reckon.

And how are your wonderful British peasants? Not giving you too much trouble, I hope!

I don't know if you've heard but there are a group of trouble makers calling themselves communists and Bolsheviks over here. They have some potty ideas about getting rid of the royal family and ruling without a Tsar. Crackers! If they think I'm going to step down and let some smelly peasant sit on my throne they've got another think coming. And if they think they can scare me with their threats then they'd better think again. You can't rattle a Romanov, my dad always used to say.

Anyway, they're having all these riots in the street. Say there's a food shortage. Can't say I've noticed it myself!

Are you having a holiday this year? To tell the truth I was hoping to pop over to Britain with the family for a bit of a break. Would next week suit you? Oh, I know the Bolsheviks will say I'm running away to save my skin. I'm not. Just fancy a trip to Britain with the wife and kids. What do you say Georgie, my dear cousin?

Look forward to hearing from you urgently – know what I mean?


All the best

Nicholas II (Emperor)

P.S. Alexandra Fyodorova sends regards.

If George had said, 'Yes,' then his cousin and the family could have been saved. What did George do?

1 Agreed to give the Russian royal family a home.

2 Refused any help.

3 Arranged for the Russian relations to get away to another safe country – but not Britain.

March 1917                                      London

Dear Cousin Nicky

Good to hear from you. Shame about your little problems with the peasants. Had a little chat with my government to see if we can help.

Sorry old chap, the answer seems to be "No". We're having enough trouble here in Britain. Seems the people don't like our old family name of Wettin because it's German. Had to change it to Windsor. So, you see, we can't afford to upset anyone. Giving sanctuary to you and the Russian family might be an invitation for the British Communists to throw us out. That would never do.

I hear they murdered your old adviser, Rasputin, that monk chappie. People are saying it will be your turn next. Utter piffle, of course. Don't worry, you should be safe. Not that you would worry. You can't rattle a Romanov, eh?

All the best

Keep the old Romanov chin up.

        George V (King)

P.S. Queen Mary sends her best wishes to you and yours.

189

**Funny fact**

**George V** was a very keen stamp collector. He was very patriotic, though. He only collected stamps from the British Empire. One day a friend phoned up with a piece of news…

George V wasn't the only monarch with time for a hobby…

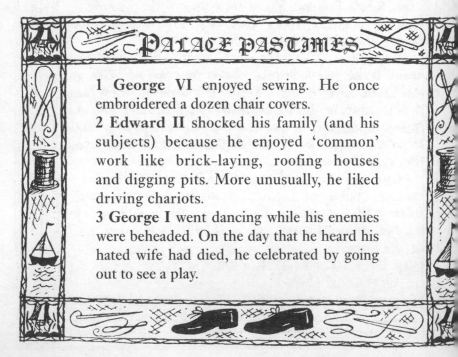

**1 George VI** enjoyed sewing. He once embroidered a dozen chair covers.

**2 Edward II** shocked his family (and his subjects) because he enjoyed 'common' work like brick-laying, roofing houses and digging pits. More unusually, he liked driving chariots.

**3 George I** went dancing while his enemies were beheaded. On the day that he heard his hated wife had died, he celebrated by going out to see a play.

**4 George V** enjoyed yachting and won many races in the yacht, *Britannia*. When George died, the family didn't want to sell the yacht – so they had it sunk.

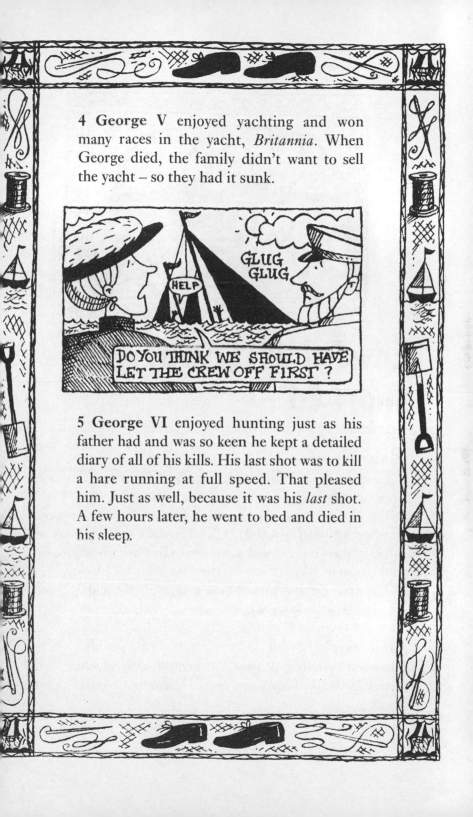

**5 George VI** enjoyed hunting just as his father had and was so keen he kept a detailed diary of all of his kills. His last shot was to kill a hare running at full speed. That pleased him. Just as well, because it was his *last* shot. A few hours later, he went to bed and died in his sleep.

# Edward VIII (1936) – Short Ed

### Claim to fame
- Came to the throne on the death of **George V** but was never crowned.
- Decided to marry an American woman, Wallis Simpson, who had been divorced. 'You can't do that and stay as king,' the Government told him. 'Give her up or give up the crown.'
- He gave up the crown (even though he hadn't been crowned, if you see what I mean).

### Funny fact
**George V** hated Edward's fashionable clothes. He especially disliked turn-ups on the bottom of trousers. One day he said…

## Foul fact

Every night **Edward**'s pug dog slept on his bed. Then, one night, the pug crept down and slept on the floor. That night Edward died. He was 77 – that's Ed, not the dog.

## Fantastic fact

In 1925, eleven years before Edward inherited the throne, a fortune-teller said this about the Prince Edward:

And that is exactly what happened. Many monarchs have believed in predictions and superstitions…

# Fascinating fateful facts

1 Halley's Comet appeared in the skies above England in the fateful year, 1066. 'A sign that the kingdom will change hands,' the wise men said. Sure enough, in that year, **King Edward the Confessor** died, **Harold** took the throne and **William the Conqueror** took it off *him* at the Battle of Hastings.

2 When **William the Conqueror** landed on the English coast and jumped ashore, he fell flat on his face. 'A bad sign,' his supporters muttered nervously. But crafty William jumped to his feet, holding on to a fistful of sand. 'See how easily I grab this land!' he cried. And he did.

3 **Stephen** went to church to pray for success before the Battle of Lincoln in 1141. As he gave a candle to the bishop, it snapped. Then a holy box (called a pyx) fell from the altar. 'A sign that King Stephen shall fall from power,' the congregation sighed. Sure enough, Stephen lost the battle.

4 **Richard II's** coronation was cursed by three accidents: he lost a coronation shoe, a gold spur fell off, then a gust of wind blew his crown off. 'A sign of an unhappy

reign to come,' the people predicted. They were right.

5 **George III** lost the great diamond from his crown on his wedding day. 'A sign that he will lose a jewel from his empire,' people predicted. And George's soldiers went on to lose the American colonies in the American War of Independence.

But no one predicted that **George VI** would become king…

# George VI (1936–1952) – Baffled Bertie

### Claim to fame

- King during the Second World War.
- Didn't expect to come to the throne because **Edward VIII** was supposed to become king.
- Like his father, he wasn't 'trained' for the throne and had a career in the navy. Found it all a strain which made him stammer in speaking – and smoke like one of his ship's chimneys.

### Fantastic fact

**George's** name was Albert – Bertie to his friends. So why didn't he become King Albert? Because Queen Victoria didn't want anyone to be called King Albert, out of respect for her dead husband.

Baby Albert Frederick Arthur George was born on the anniversary of Prince Albert's death … but Victoria forgave Bertie's father for this clumsy accident … and allowed him to be named after her husband. When he became king he chose to use one of his other names.

**Funny fact**

Bertie joined the navy. At Naval College he took the exams and came 68th. This was not very impressive. There were only 68 in the class.

LOOK ON THE BRIGHT SIDE ... AT LEAST YOU WERE TOP ROYAL!

*Did you know…?*

1 Buckingham Palace was bombed during the Second World War. **George VI** was sure that the bomber was his Spanish cousin, the Duke of Galliera, because he was an ace pilot … and he knew the way to Buckingham Palace. (So does every tourist with a simple map, of course, but George didn't consider that argument.) The queen said, 'I'm glad we've been bombed.' She felt they were sharing the suffering of their people. But some of their people weren't too impressed – the blitzed Londoners, unlike George and Elizabeth, didn't have another couple of palaces to go off to.

2 Bertie wanted Elizabeth Bowes-Lyon to marry him. He tried for two-and-a-half years. She always said, 'No.' Then he tried asking her personally – for two-and-a-half years

he'd been sending messengers to ask. Once he asked for himself she said, 'Yes.'

As you'll remember, **George VI** was the first British monarch to visit America. That's just one of the incredible things you'll never need to know about British monarchs … but you can use it to show off to parents, teachers, friends or visiting orang-utans. Here are some more…

# Did you know…?

Amaze, astound and bore your teachers by telling them this trivia…

**1 Henry VII** was the only British monarch to be crowned on the field of battle.

**2 Victoria** was the first British monarch ever to travel in a train.

**3** In all, 125 people were beheaded in the Tower of London.

**4** The Tower of London was used in the First World War to house German spies – 11 were shot at the Tower.

**5 George V** was the first monarch to make a radio broadcast.

**6 Lady Jane Grey** was so tiny she was probably the only monarch to go to her coronation wearing platform shoes.

**7** Nine days later, **Lady Jane Grey** became the shortest-ruling monarch (and also the shortest) when she lost her head. Lady Jane Grey was pronounced Queen of two countries

– England and Ireland. But only two *towns* accepted her. For just nine short days, she was Queen of Berwick and King's Lynn.

8 **Mary Queen of Scots** had a watch in the shape of a human skull.

9 **Edward VII's** wife, **Queen Alexandra**, became very eccentric in her old age. She lived at Sandringham House in Norfolk and every day would go out for a drive in her carriage. She would graciously wave and bow her head to the cows in the fields as she passed.

10 All six of **Henry VIII's** wives were related to each other.

# Elizabeth II (1952–present) – Lizzie the Last

## Claim to fame

- Doesn't consider the Windsors a *family* so much as a *business*.

- Perhaps one of the richest women in the UK, yet British people pay her millions every year to be queen. But she has also opened Buckingham Palace to paying tourists in 1993 – to help make enough cash to repair fire damage at Windsor Castle.
- All four of her children have been married and three have been divorced. Usual average for miserable monarchic marriages!
- She's a record holder. Not only is she Britain's longest-ruling monarch, but she's also the only monarch to have celebrated a Sapphire Jubilee. Marking a whopping 65 years on the throne.

## Mean queen

As a child, **Elizabeth II** was nicknamed Lilibet – because that was the way her baby tongue tried to pronounce her own name. Her governess reported that Lilibet and her sister, Margaret, could fight ... viciously:

**Funny fact**

The present Prince of Wales is **Prince Charles**. He has rather large ears. In June 1994 he went to Caernarfon to celebrate 25 years as Prince of Wales. The local joke shop almost sold out of joke big ears – Windsor Wingnuts as they called them. They also had 'Prince Charles masks' in the window. The local police said they were 'disrespectful' and ordered that they be kept under the counter. The owner was threatened with arrest but still refused to remove the ears. In the end, the police went away – the ears stayed.

**Test your teacher**

The **Prince of Wales** asked **Lady Diana Spencer** to marry him. She said, 'No.' True or false?

> *Answer:* If your teacher says 'True', then *you* say 'False' – the son of **Elizabeth II**, **Prince Charles**, asked **Lady Diana Spencer** to marry him in 1980. She said, 'Yes.' If your teacher says 'False' then you say it's 'True' – the son of **George I**, Prince George, asked Lady Diana Spencer to marry him in the 1730s. She said, 'No.'

**Fantastic fact**

The Queen's oldest son married Diana, the late **Princess of Wales**. But did you know that she was related to *all four* of Henry VIII's English wives?

**Foul fact**

**Elizabeth II's** castle of Sandringham is haunted at Christmas. Each Christmas Eve, the Christmas cards are thrown to the floor. (Of course, it could simply be a very draughty castle.)

# Epilogue

**Elizabeth II** calls the royal family 'The Firm'. But 'The Firm' is in the business of selling 'Royalty' ... and not so many people seem to want it these days. When you look at some of the cruel kings and mean queens the Brits have had in the last thousand years, it's not too surprising really.

Let's be honest, Britain has been pretty unlucky with its kings and queens. There have been mad ones, bad ones, greedy ones and cruel ones. Some have been all these things at the same time!

The Brits have had their share of murdering, mutilating and misruling monarchs.

Do we want any more?

The amazing answer is, 'Probably – yes!'

Britain got rid of the monarchy once before when **Charles I** got the chop. But it was so BORING without a king and queen, the Brits brought back Chopped Charlie's son to rule again.

Would the same thing happen again if we got rid of **Elizabeth II** and the royal family? What would the newspapers have to write about if there weren't royal scandals and shocking secrets? Whose face could we stick on stamps and five-pound notes? Who could we give the millions of pounds that we pay the Royals to be … well, royal?

The Royals are as useless as they ever were … but the Brits seem to like them that way. We've had cruel kings and mean queens for about a thousand years now – we'll probably have them for another thousand.

## Who said that?

Of all the monarchs in all the palaces in all of Britain, which one said…

THERE'S TOO MUCH YOU KNOW, HISTORY